Wildflowers
of the
Tahoe Sierra

D1474960

WILD*flowers*
of the
Tahoe Sierra

From Forest Deep to Mountain Peak

Laird R. Blackwell

THE PUBLISHER: LONE PINE PUBLISHING

16149 Redmond Way, #180	206, 10426-81 Avenue	202A, 1110 Seymour Street
Redmond, Washington	Edmonton, Alberta	Vancouver, British Columbia
USA 98052	Canada T6E 1X5	Canada V6B 3N3

Canadian Cataloguing in Publication Data
Blackwell, Laird R. (Laird Richard), 1945–
  Wildflowers of the Tahoe Sierra

  Includes bibliographical references and index.
  ISBN 1-55105-085-4

  1. Wild flowers—Tahoe, Lake, Region (Calif. and Nev.)—
Identification. 2. Wild flowers—Tahoe, Lake, Region (Calif.
and Nev.)—Pictorial works. I. Title.
QK149.B62 1997   582.13'09794'38   C96-910853-2

Senior Editor: Nancy Foulds
Editor: Roland Lines
Production Manager: David Dodge
Design, layout and production: Gregory Brown
Photography: Laird R. Blackwell
Separations and Film: Elite Lithographers, Edmonton, Alberta, Canada
Printing: Quebecor Jasper Printing, Edmonton, Alberta, Canada

The publisher gratefully acknowledges the support of Alberta
Community Development and the Department of Canadian Heritage.

CONTENTS

For Melinda, my mountain wildflower
and love of my life, in celebration of our
passionate and loving journey through
the joys and beauties of this wonder-filled world.

In the tiniest bud is a world

bursting to be known;

Crushing a sapling or blocking a soul

is a hundred worlds dying.

ACKNOWLEDGMENTS

Warm thanks to all my companions, friends, and students over the years who have helped me discover and celebrate the joys of the mountains and their wildflower creatures.

Thanks also to Steve Matson, president of the Tahoe Chapter of the California Native Plant Society, for his helpful review of the text, and to the staff of Lone Pine Publishing, for their support, encouragement, and careful and respectful editing. It's exciting and gratifying to see an inner vision be born into form and substance.

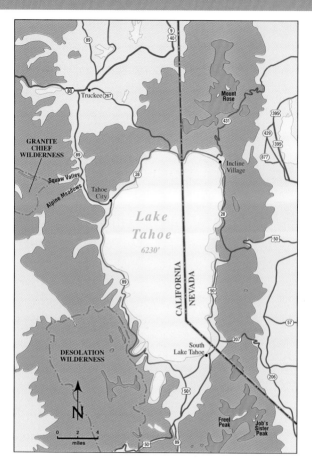

Life Zone	Elev. Range
Alpine (Arctic)	above 10,500'
Subalpine (Hudsonian)	9000'–10,500'
Red Fir (Canadian)	6500'–9000'
Yellow Pine (Transitional)	6200'–6500'

INTRODUCTION

A HIKER WITH EVEN THE most casual interest in wildflowers cannot help but notice the exceptional variety and beauty of the flowers in the Tahoe mountains. Tahoe provides a marvelous variety of special environments: elevations range from 6200' to almost 10,900'; there is a mixture of granitic and volcanic rock; and habitats vary from deep forests to open, windswept ridges, and from snow-fed meadows to dry, sun-baked slopes. Montane plants from the Yosemite Sierra to the south and the Cascades to the north mix with high-desert migrants from the Great Basin to the east and indigenous California plants from the foothills to the west to produce a rich Tahoe flora of over 1200 species.

The purpose of this book is to introduce you to some of the most beautiful, interesting, frequent, and infrequent wildflowers you may encounter while hiking in Tahoe. This book is a handy field guide to identifying wildflowers, and it is an introduction to the ecology of plants, as it puts great emphasis on the relationship between plants and their environment.

Many aspects of topography and climate interact to create special micro-environments that support unique associations of plants. Elevation (especially very high elevation) has a significant influence on vegetation types, but local moisture, temperature, and soil conditions are usually even more important; variations in local environments can create different plants communities at the same elevations.

The Tahoe life zones and their approximate elevation ranges are as follows:

Yellow Pine (Transitional): 6200' to 6500'
Red Fir (Canadian): 6500' to 9000'
Subalpine (Hudsonian): 9000' to 10,500'
Alpine (Arctic): above 10,500'

The wildflower descriptions in this book are organized into chapters according to the following environmental types:
1) deep forests and partly shaded forest clearings
2) rock ledges and talus and scree slopes
3) ponds and small lake edges
4) wet meadows, streambanks, and seeps
5) dry, open slopes and flats
6) grassy meadows and other damp-to-dryish areas
7) alpine slopes, ridges, and peaks (above timberline).

The introduction to each chapter describes the unique characteristics of that environment and of the plants that live there. The individual plant descriptions include identifying characteristics, interesting features, global and local distributions, and descriptions of related plants. Each description is accompanied by a photograph that is intended to help in identification and to give some idea of the flower's special beauty.

I hope you will find the discussions and photographs of the wildflowers interesting enough to make this book fun to read and study. If you also take this book out in the field, there are a few different ways you can use it to help identify flowers:

1) Simply thumb through the photographs.
2) Turn to the chapter for the type of environment you are in, and look through the photographs and descriptions. (Distinguishing characteristics are in **boldface** type).
3) Use the quick-reference table (pp. 130–33), which groups the species with similar flowers according to the color, number, and arrangement of the petals.

Of course, if you think you know the flower's name (common or scientific), you can refer to the appropriate index. There is also a listing of the flower families included in this book. You might want to compare the different flowers in each family; it's a good way to get to know the plant families and their identifying characteristics.

Names (common or scientific) are, of course, human impositions on the flowers. As such, they are 2-edged swords: they can help us come to know a flower as an individual personality and a friend, and to understand its relationship to other flowers; but they can also come between us and knowing the flower—we may get so attached to the labels that we no longer see or even look at the flowers themselves. I encourage you to get to know the names, but still to truly encounter the flowers as you meet them—there is always more to experience and learn about a flower!

Another caution about names: scientific names are not completely reliable and unchanging. Genus, species, and even family names may be different in different botanical texts. Sometimes botanists disagree; more often some of the names are changed with time. I have tried to use the scientific names in widest use, while including in the text and in the indexes the most recent changes (such as those indicated in *The Jepson Manual of Higher Plants of California* [Hickman 1993]).

Just a note about the proper treatment of wildflowers. The old adage 'take nothing but pictures (and memories), leave nothing but footprints' needs some elaboration. Although I strongly discourage picking any wildflowers, I can understand why some people want to. If you feel that you must pick flowers, please be certain that you really want to. Wildflowers fade very quickly after being picked, and I've seen so many wilted wildflowers discarded along trails. Photographs, drawings, careful notes, and memories may be more satisfying—especially for the flowers! Pick flowers, if you must, only when there are many of the same flowers in the area. Don't pick all the flowers from one plant, and **never** pull a plant up by the roots. Of course, wildflower picking is **never** allowed in national parks.

Plants are quite rugged, but you can do considerable damage if you tramp through a marshy meadow. Although it may not be as obvious, the sparse and rocky soil above timberline is also extremely fragile: just by kicking loose a few rocks you can deprive a plant of needed shelter or tear loose roots that have been struggling for perhaps hundreds of years to survive. Stay on the trails, walk carefully, and enjoy the wildflowers in a way that respects their lives and leaves them intact.

Although this book focuses on the wildflowers of Tahoe, many of the flowers discussed here can be found throughout the Sierra Nevada, and some even extend into the Cascades.

DEEP FORESTS &
PARTLY SHADED FOREST CLEARINGS

MUCH OF TAHOE IS HEAVILY forested. Yellow Pine forests of ponderosa pine, white fir, and incense cedar are common in a narrow band near Lake Tahoe (6200' to 6500'). Dense Red Fir forests, consisting primarily of Jeffrey pine, lodgepole pine, and red fir, dominate the area from a few hundred feet above Lake Tahoe to near the summits of all but the highest peaks (from 6500' to 9000'). Subalpine forests of whitebark pine, western white pine, Sierra juniper, and mountain hemlock struggle near timberline on the higher peaks (9000' to 10,500').

Of course, forests don't cover all the natural landscape from lake level to timberline; local conditions of topography, moisture, exposure, and soil can create micro-environments where forests can't survive. Later chapters will discuss these non-forest habitats and their wildflowers. This chapter will introduce you to some of the fascinating wildflowers of the woods.

With limited sunlight, it is not always possible for plants to photosynthesize enough food. Some green-leaf plants supplement their photosynthesis by digesting decaying organic matter or living material from neighboring plants; non-green plants don't photosynthesize, and so obtain **all** their food from other plants.

Adaptations for survival in the shade have produced some unusual and intriguing flowers that are well worth seeking. Whether by bright or unusual colors, odd leaves or bracts, or considerable height, most of the wildflowers of the deep forest are anything but subtle or camouflaged.

Most plants of deep forest will tend
on others for food to depend.
Green life in the sun
they emphatically shun,
preferring to dine on a friend.

PINEDROPS
Pterospora andromedea ❦ *Wintergreen Family*

Pinedrops is one of several Tahoe forest plants that do not photosynthesize their own food. Pinedrops first appears as a fleshy, sticky, velvety pink shoot that pushes through the forest litter. It grows into a **1–4', reddish-brown, clammy stalk**, from which many small, white, urn-shaped flowers hang. The 'leaves,' which are not needed for photosynthesis, are reduced to reddish-brown scales. After one summer of growth and flowering, the stalk dies and dries to a dark reddish-brown color. It often remains standing for years, a slightly ominous reminder of the shortness of the bloom.

Pinedrops is limited to rich humus in Yellow Pine and Red Fir forests.

DEEP FORESTS • WHITE FLOWERS • 5 PETALS, UNITED IN AN URN

RANGE: Fairly common throughout the mountain forests of North America.
TAHOE LOCATIONS: Fairly common in dense forests up to about 8000'.

WHITE-VEINED WINTERGREEN
Pyrola picta ∽ *Wintergreen Family*

Unlike the forest plants that produce none of their own food, wintergreens are only partially parasitic or mycotrophic. As the common name indicates, these plants are not only green-leaved, but they also retain their leaves all year round. This tactic gives a considerable advantage to plants with limited access to sunlight: the leaves are completely formed and ready to photosynthesize as soon as the snow melts in the spring.

White-veined wintergreen is 6–12" tall. It has waxy, white flowers with sharply bent styles that protrude from the cup of the upside-down flowers. White-veined wintergreen is a 'weather recorder': it has somewhat leathery **basal leaves with very distinctive white veins**, and the width of the white veins shrinks with increased sun exposure (because more chlorophyll is produced in the leaves for photosynthesis).

Related plants: One-sided wintergreen (*Pyrola secunda*) has all its flowers hanging from one side of the stem. **Bog wintergreen** (*P. asarifolia*) has a tall stalk of pink flowers, and it grows in wet areas (as the name suggests).

FOREST OPENINGS • WHITE FLOWERS
5 SEPARATE PETALS, FORMING A BOWL

RANGE: Throughout the western mountains.
TAHOE LOCATIONS: Frequent in forests up to about 9000'.

PIPSISSEWA, LITTLE PRINCE'S PINE
Chimaphila menziesii ∾ *Wintergreen Family*

Like the wintergreens (p. 15), pipsissewa has evergreen leaves. It bears a superficial resemblance to the wintergreens: it has leathery, shiny leaves, which are sometimes mottled with white; its stem is thin and erect; and it has waxy, hanging, white flowers. Pipsissewa flowers are much more open than the cup-like wintergreen flowers, however, and they **resemble crowns**. Also, pipsissewa **leaves have small teeth** and occur on the stem as well as at the base of the plant.

The genus name *Chimaphila* (winter-loving) refers to the evergreen nature of the leaves. The species name *menziesii* honors Archibald Menzies, a Scottish naturalist. The common name 'pipsissewa' is thought to be derived from a Cree word meaning 'it breaks into small pieces,' because this plant was used by them in a mixture to dissolve gall stones and kidney stones.

Some botanists merge the wintergreen family into the heath family, but others separate the urn-flowered plants that live in the deep shade into their own family (wintergreen) as I've chosen to do.

**FORESTS • WHITE FLOWERS
5 SEPARATE PETALS, FORMING A CROWN**

RANGE: Throughout the western mountains.
TAHOE LOCATIONS: Occasional in shade up to about 7500'.

SPOTTED CORALROOT
Corallorhiza maculata ∽ Orchid Family

The remarkable diversity of parasitic and saprophytic plants in the Sierra Nevada probably arises from the relative warmth and moisture of the moderate winter temperatures and heavy snow cover, which are ideal for root fungal activity. One of the more uncommon of these types of plants is spotted coralroot, a mycotrophic orchid.

Spotted coralroot has a 1–3', red-purple or yellowish stalk, from which branch several orchid-like flowers. It gets its name from the **showy, white lower petal of its flower, which is covered with small purple spots.** The rest of the flower (two other petals and three sepals) is the same reddish color as the stalk.

Corallorhiza means 'coral root,' and it refers to the thick, much-branched root, which resembles brain coral (or so I've read). This plant is rare, so **do not** dig one up!

Related plants: Broad-lipped twayblade (*Listera convallarioides*) is an odd yellow-green orchid with opposite leaves and small flowers with 'shovel-like' lower lips. It is rare in Tahoe.

**DEEP FORESTS • WHITE FLOWERS WITH MAROON SPOTS
6 SEPARATE 'PETALS' (3 ARE ACTUALLY SEPALS)**

RANGE: Throughout the American West and East.
TAHOE LOCATIONS: Infrequent in deep forest up to about 7500'.

STAR TULIP
Calochortus nudus ⚬ *Lily Family*

The delicate star tulip is one of the gorgeous mariposa lilies of Tahoe. It grows in forest clearings and is considerably less common than Leichtlin's mariposa lily (p. 74), which grows in dry areas.

One or a few satiny, white to lavender, 3-petaled flowers sit atop a 4–12" stem. **A lone grass-like leaf** rises nearly vertically, extending above the flowers, and seeming to offer them protection.

Although Tahoe has some beautiful mariposa lilies—'mariposa' means 'butterfly'—the Sierra Nevada foothills are mariposa heaven: they sport many species with yellow, white, or pink flowers—some smooth and silky, and others densely bearded.

The species name *nudus* refers to the fact that the flower is on a stem that is nearly naked of leaves.

**FOREST OPENINGS • WHITE TO LAVENDER FLOWERS
3 SEPARATE PETALS, ALL ALIKE**

RANGE: The mountains of California and southwestern Oregon.
TAHOE LOCATIONS: Rare in forest openings up to about 8500'.

In a family with unusual flowers, meadow rue is certainly no exception. The flowers have no petals, and the four or five sepals drop off early in the summer, leaving just the reproductive parts. A flower without petals or sepals for most of the season is likely to either have colorful stamens (to attract pollinators) or to be wind pollinated. Both are true for meadow rue.

An individual Fendler's meadow rue plant has flowers of only one sex. **The dainty male flowers have drooping clusters of many greenish and yellow stamens. The female flowers have many thick, close-packed, erect, greenish pistils**. This tall (2–5'), slender plant has branches near its base that bear delicate, 3-lobed leaves; the smaller branches above carry many of the odd flowers.

Related plants: Few-flowered meadow rue (*Thalictrum sparsiflorum*) occurs occasionally in Tahoe meadows. Though you will recognize it as a meadow rue, its flowers have both male and female parts.

FOREST OPENINGS • GREENISH
TO YELLOWISH FLOWERS • NO PETALS

RANGE: Common in much of the West.
TAHOE LOCATIONS: Common in forest openings up to about 8500'.

DWARF LOUSEWORT, PINEWOODS LOUSEWORT
Pedicularis semibarbata ∞ *Snapdragon Family*

Dwarf lousewort grows in the partial shade of small openings in Yellow Pine and Red Fir forests. This plant thereby receives somewhat more sunlight than the plants of deep forest, and consequently produces all its food by photosynthesis. Dwarf lousewort has **large, fern-like leaves** that lie nearly flat on the ground, **partially concealing the yellow tube flowers,** which grow on very short (1–4") stems.

As in other members of the snapdragon family, the lousewort flower is a 2-lipped tube with two petals in the upper lip and three in the lower lip. In dwarf lousewort, the upper two petals unite to form a short beak.

The species name *semibarbata* means 'half-bearded,' in reference to the fuzzy, white hair found at the tip of the flower tube.

FOREST OPENINGS • YELLOW FLOWERS
5 PETALS, UNITED IN A 2-LIPPED TUBE

RANGE: Southern Oregon to southern California.
TAHOE LOCATIONS: Common in partially shaded forest openings up to about 8500'.

CRIMSON COLUMBINE
Aquilegia formosa ☙ Buttercup Family

Like California fuchsia (p. 35), crimson columbine is an ideal hummingbird flower; it has long, thin nectar spurs and bright red (or orange) blossoms. (Birds see red, but most insects do not—their spectrum of visible light is shifted to the blue end and beyond to the ultraviolet.)

As with most other members of the buttercup family, crimson columbine has petal-like sepals and many stamens. The five flaring, red 'petals' are actually the sepals: **the petals are yellow at the tip and extend back into long red spurs.** Many of the large (2"), showy **flowers hang upside-down** along the tall (to 3' or so) stems, becoming upright when they go to fruit. The leaves are divided into three scalloped leaflets.

Related plants: The much larger **alpine columbine** (*Aquilegia pubescens*), which does not occur as far north as Lake Tahoe, sometimes occurs together with crimson columbine near timberline. Alpine columbine is white, however, and its nectar spurs point down (making it much more attractive and convenient for the sphinx moth, which does not visit crimson columbine). Hybrids of these two columbines sometimes occur (bees will pierce the nectar tubes and steal the nectar from both species, occasionally bumping the sex organs and transferring pollen from one species to the other!). To see these remarkable hybrids—large pinkish-white flowers at a 45° angle on the stem—is a rare and moving experience; they are as beautiful as they are infrequent.

**FOREST OPENINGS • RED TO ORANGE FLOWERS
5 SEPARATE PETALS, EACH WITH A LONG NECTAR SPUR**

RANGE: Common in many environments throughout the West.
TAHOE LOCATIONS: Common in open woods up to about 9500'.

21

SNOWPLANT
Sarcodes sanguinea ∽ *Wintergreen Family*

   The intensely red snowplant is probably the most dazzling of the forest's flowering plants. Its fleshy, **asparagus-like shoots** push up through the forest floor litter to a height of 1' or more. Although Native Americans commonly gathered it for food, because of its startling beauty and relative rarity it was one of the first plants in California to be protected by law; there is a heavy fine for picking or damaging it.

   Although snowplant does not normally grow up through the snow, it probably gets its common name from the fact that it is one of the earliest plants to appear and bloom: it usually pushes up its thick red stem in May, in the wake of retreating snowbanks. When snowplant first appears, the red, strap-like 'leaves' are wrapped tightly around the stalk tip. It is not until later that the **tightly packed, hanging, urn-shaped, red flowers** emerge from between the covering bracts.

Its deep shade environment should lead you to wonder how snowplant could receive enough sunlight to photosynthesize its food. The lack of green leaves (or green anywhere on the plant for that matter) tells you that this plant doesn't photosynthesize at all; instead, snowplant is saprophytic, obtaining its nutrients from decaying organic matter in the rich forest humus. 'Mycotrophic' (obtaining nutrients from fungus) is technically a more accurate term, because recent research has shown that the roots actually parasitize the soil fungi that coat them. These root fungi get their food by breaking down decaying matter or by parasitizing the roots of neighboring trees and shrubs. In any case, snowplant thrives in deep shade by obtaining nourishment from other plant matter, rather than by producing it itself.

The scientific name for snowplant is quite descriptive: *Sarcodes* means 'fleshy,' and *sanguinea* means 'blood-red.'

DEEP FORESTS • RED FLOWERS • 5 PETALS, UNITED IN AN URN

RANGE: Limited in distribution to Yellow Pine and Red Fir forests from southern California to southern Oregon. It is fairly commonly seen in those areas (especially around Tahoe), but it is still protected by law.
TAHOE LOCATIONS: Common in deep forests up to about 8000'.

ROCK LEDGES &
TALUS & SCREE SLOPES

THE SIERRA NEVADA IS RENOWNED for its massive, smooth slabs and cliffs of shining white granite. In Tahoe, especially in its northern portion, there are also a considerable number of volcanic peaks, sometimes occurring side-by-side with granitic ones. These 'contact' areas are often strikingly dramatic, for the rich reds, oranges, and rusts of crumbly volcanic rock contrast sharply with the slick gleam of the granitic rock.

While the deep forest environment is difficult for plants because of the limited sunlight, the rocky mountain environment is difficult because of limited water and soil. In many places from lake level up to timberline, the pine and fir forests are interrupted by rock slabs, ledges, boulder fields, and slopes of loose rock (talus) or gravel (scree), where there is insufficient moisture and soil for the growth of forests. The conditions in these dry, rocky areas—shallow or nonexistent soil, little water retention, unstable slopes, high reflectance of light and re-radiation of heat—present a dry, inhospitable environment in which only a few wildflowers with special adaptations can survive. In this environment, you will often find plants with succulent or waxy leaves to reduce water loss and with long, tough roots to find deep water and to provide anchorage. Flexible and quickly growing roots are also advantageous in responding to shifting slopes of loose rock.

Above timberline, much of the terrain is also rocky or gravelly, but for the plants that live exclusively or primarily in this 'alpine' environment, rocky soil is only one of the many severe environmental conditions they have to endure (see chapter 7, p. 115).

Plants on hot rocks can get fried,
and without their thick leaves they'd be dried;
while a plant in steep scree
might quite suddenly break free
and just be along for the ride.

DRUMMOND'S ANEMONE, WINDFLOWER
Anemone drummondii ⁀ *Buttercup Family*

One of the rarer of Tahoe wildflowers and one of the few members of the buttercup family to thrive outside a wet environment, Drummond's anemone is found (if you're lucky) early in the season on dry, rocky slopes and flats. Typical of its family in appearance, it has a varying number of petal-like sepals (it has no true petals) and a central clump of many stamens and pistils. The five to eight egg-shaped sepals overlap to form either a flat wheel or a bowl. They are **white, often with a gorgeous deep blue tinge on their undersides**.

The genus name *Anemone* and the common name 'windflower' both allude to what happens when the plant goes to seed. The flower becomes a round, densely woolly head whose many seeds are easily carried away on the fall winds.

**ROCKY SLOPES AND FLATS • WHITE FLOWERS
5–8 SEPARATE 'PETALS' (ACTUALLY SEPALS)**

RANGE: Throughout the West.
TAHOE LOCATIONS: Rare on rocky slopes and flats up to about 8500'.

The buckwheat genus (*Eriogonum*) has more than 300 species, most of which grow in the western United States. At least 12 species can be found in Tahoe. It is often hard to distinguish between species, but Lobb's buckwheat is distinctive for its **long, prostrate stems**. Like most buckwheats, the end of each stem bears a large, round flowerhead that is densely packed with tiny crepe-paper flowers. Each flower has six tiny, petal-like sepals that are creamy white, fading to rose. The 2–8" stems are unusual in that they lie flat on the ground. The oval leaves are white-woolly and form a basal rosette.

Related plants: Nude buckwheat (*E. nudum*) has large, spherical, white flowerheads atop tall, leafless stems. It is found in dry areas. **Dirty socks** (*Polygonum bistortoides*) grows in very wet areas, and it has cylindrical, white flowerheads that smell just like … dirty socks!

ROCKY SLOPES AND LEDGES • CREAMY WHITE FLOWERS, IN DENSE BALLS • 6 TINY 'PETALS' (ACTUALLY SEPALS)

RANGE: The mountains of California and western Nevada.
TAHOE LOCATIONS: Common on rocky, gravelly slopes from about 7000' to the highest summits above timberline.

MOUNTAIN SORREL
Oxyria digyna ∞ *Buckwheat Family*

Mountain sorrel is a delightful plant that is as appreciated for its pert appearance and tart-tasting leaves as it is admired for its tenacity in surviving its harsh, rocky environment. Mountain sorrel has tenacious roots that can provide anchorage and find water in difficult circumstances. They can also sprout offshoots remarkably quickly. Mountain sorrel is a 'pioneer' plant in rocky mountain terrain.

Though its flowers are very tiny, the lush, thick, **kidney-shaped basal leaves and the clusters of greenish flowers** along the 2–15" stems make this plant very noticeable and attractive, especially when it is found, as it often is, **clinging precariously to a vertical slab of bare rock** or nestling in the middle of a treacherous scree slope. Mountain sorrel blooms late into the fall, when it becomes even more noticeable as the tiny greenish flowers turn into clumps of equally tiny red seed capsules.

The genus name *Oxyria*, from the Greek for 'sour,' refers to the sour, acidic taste of the leaves.

ROCK WALLS AND SLOPES • WHITE TO GREENISH FLOWERS, IN CLUSTERS • 4–6 TINY 'PETALS' (ACTUALLY SEPALS)

RANGE: Circumboreal; throughout the mountains of the Northern Hemisphere from the Arctic to Eurasia and across North America.
TAHOE LOCATIONS: Occasional in rock crevices and scree slopes from about 7000' to 10,300'.

MOUNTAIN SHIELDLEAF
MOUNTAIN JEWELFLOWER
Streptanthus tortuosus ∽ *Mustard Family*

An especially striking member of the mustard family is the common mountain shieldleaf. It is easily recognized as a mustard by the arrangement of the petals and the shape of the seed pods: the small flowers have four petals arranged in a cross; the seed pods are thin, papery and long (2–6"). Many flowers branch off along the upper part of the 8–36" stem. The sepals are purplish, and they close into a twisted 'vase,' in which the small, white-to-pink petals are held. Along the lower part of the stem are this plant's most distinctive feature—its leaves. They are **thick and roundish (shield-like), and they turn bronze or golden late in the season.** The leaves grow completely around the stem (an arrangement called 'perfoliate'), and they occur every inch or so on the lower stem. The effect is a shish kabob of leaves on a skewer.

Whoever named this plant wanted to emphasize its 'twisted' nature; both its genus and species names refer to this characteristic.

Related plants: Though it is from a different family (purslane) and grows in a different environment (grassy meadows), **miner's lettuce** (*Montia perfoliata*, also called *Claytonia perfoliata*) has somewhat similar perfoliate leaves surrounding the plant stem.

ROCKY FLATS AND SLOPES • WHITE, PINK, OR PURPLE FLOWERS • 4 SEPARATE PETALS

RANGE: Only in the mountains of northern California and southwestern Oregon.
TAHOE LOCATIONS: Common on dry, rocky slopes from lake level to about 10,200'.

PINK ALUM-ROOT
Heuchera rubescens ∾ Saxifrage Family

One of the daintiest of the mountain plants, pink alum-root appears all the more delicate in contrast to its rugged rock environment. From clumps of lobed, rounded, rock-hugging basal leaves rise **several tall, slender stems, from which branch clusters of tiny, cup-shaped, white to pink flowers that quiver in the slightest breeze**.

The scientific family name Saxifragaceae means 'rock-breaker,' which reflects the adaptations of many members of this family (including alum-root) to harsh rocky environments. The strong roots of these plants are able to penetrate into the smallest of rock cracks, sometimes crumbling the rock in the process. Also, some Native Americans ground up many saxifrage family plants to make a potion to dissolve kidney stones and gallstones.

**ROCK LEDGES AND CREVICES • WHITE TO PINK FLOWERS
5 TINY SEPARATE PETALS**

RANGE: Only in the mountains of California and western Nevada.
TAHOE LOCATIONS: Occasional on rock ledges and in crevices from about 6800' to 9500'.

One of the earliest-blooming Tahoe wildflowers, and one of the most difficult to find, is the 'beastly' steershead, which does **bear a striking resemblance to a steer's skull** … complete with horns! The $1/2$" flower is white or pastel pink, and the two inner petals join to create the main part of the 'skull,' while the two outer petals curve back to form the 'horns.'

Although steershead often grows in large clusters, it is difficult to see because of its small size and because its color blends remarkably well with its gravelly or sandy habitat. When you do find it, you may find yourself suddenly parched and reaching for your water bottle, for this amazing flower looks for all the world like a sun-bleached steer's skull you would find in the middle of the Mojave Desert. Each 1–4" stem has only one flower at its tip and no leaves; the deeply lobed leaves grow on their own stems, which are attached with the flower stems to the underground root cluster.

Botanists have recently moved all genera of the fumitory family into the poppy family.

**ROCKY OR SANDY FLATS • WHITE TO PINK FLOWERS
4 PETALS, UNITED IN AN IRREGULAR SHAPE**

RANGE: Northern California to Washington; east to Utah and Wyoming.
TAHOE LOCATIONS: Rare on open, gravelly or sandy flats
up to about 9000'.

BUSH CINQUEFOIL
Potentilla fruticosa ⁓ *Rose Family*

Bush cinquefoil is **the only cinquefoil that is a shrub**, but its flowers are nonetheless very much like the typical yellow cinquefoil bloom. Each ¹/₂–1" flower consists of five separate petals around a central cluster of many reproductive parts. The flowers occur in small clusters atop the 1–4' shrub, which is thick and has short, gray-green leaflets.

The genus name *Potentilla* refers to the 'potent' medicinal qualities of these plants.

Related plants: Five-finger cinquefoil (*P. gracilis*) has compound leaves of five to seven palmate leaflets. **Sticky cinquefoil** (*P. glandulosa*) has pinnately compound leaves and whitish flowers.

ROCKY SLOPES AND FLATS
YELLOW FLOWERS • 5 SEPARATE PETALS

RANGE: Circumboreal; widespread across the Northern Hemisphere.
TAHOE LOCATIONS: Occasional on rocky, open slopes up to about 9000'.

NARROW-PETALED STONECROP
Sedum lanceolatum ~ *Stonecrop Family*

One of the adaptations to an environment where water is hard to come by is 'succulence'—having fleshy tissues that retain moisture. Stonecrops have **thick, fleshy leaves** that contain a sticky sap that is slow to evaporate. Also, the leaves are noticeably waxy, and their pores open only in the cool of the night to admit carbon dioxide, which is stored for daytime use in photosynthesis.

As the species name *lanceolatum* indicates, this stonecrop has narrow, pointed (lance-shaped) leaves. The leaves occur on the stem and in a tight **rosette** at the base of the plant. Rosettes are effective (and exquisitely beautiful) adaptations to environments where evaporation is a problem: through the intricate staggering of the leaves (much like the rows of seats in a movie theater), each leaf is exposed to the sun but is nearly flat on the ground, away from the desiccating wind.

The **5-petaled, star-shaped, yellow flowers** sit at the tips of the 2–8" stems. The stems usually grow in large clusters, in part because the plant reproduces vegetatively as well as sexually, sprouting new stems from old, fallen stems that lie intact over the winter.

Related plants: Sierra stonecrop (*Sedum obtusatum*), which has spoon-shaped leaves, also grows in rocky areas.

ROCKY LEDGES • YELLOW FLOWERS
5 PETALS, UNITED AT THE BASE TO FORM A TUBE

RANGE: Widespread through the western mountains.
TAHOE LOCATIONS: Occasional on rock ledges up to about 10,000'.

ROSY SEDUM
WESTERN ROSEROOT, KING'S CROWN
Sedum roseum ➣ *Stonecrop Family*

Although it is another of the succulent stonecrops that grow in rocky areas, rosy sedum bears only a slight resemblance to the two yellow-flowered stonecrops (p. 33). The most obvious differences are in the color and shape of the flowers: **the flowers of rosy sedum are red and have only four (rarely five) petals** that are separate only at the tips, the greater part being united into an urn-shaped tube. Because the flowers are smaller, and because the 2–12" stems are thick with leaves, the flowers of this plant are less conspicuous than those of the other sedums. Nonetheless, the overall effect of the great mass of deep red flowers displayed against the lush green, fleshy leaves is dazzling.

The species name *roseum* may refer to the color of the flowers, but as one of the common names (roseroot) suggests, it may refer to the rose-like fragrance of the roots.

ROCKY FLATS • RED FLOWERS
4 SEPARATE PETALS, UNITED IN A TUBE

RANGE: Circumboreal; throughout much of the Northern Hemisphere.
TAHOE LOCATIONS: Occasional in rocky areas from about 7000' to 10,500'.

Zauschneria californica ~ *Evening-primrose Family*

Toward the end of summer, the soft straw-browns of seed pods and drying stems replace the earlier blazes of wildflower color. But amid this delicate and subtle fall landscape, on and about barren rock ledges, appear **great masses of scarlet trumpets**—the large flowers of California fuchsia, whose strong, penetrating roots allow it to pioneer in the sparse soil of rock habitats. As it is one of the last Tahoe wildflowers to bloom, California fuchsia is a wonderful source of nectar for hummingbirds on their southward fall migration.

Although California fuchsia resembles the tubular penstemons (p. 38), it is easily distinguished by **having only four petals, each of which is 2-lobed** (as is frequent in the evening-primrose family).

California fuschia is given the scientific name *Epilobium canum* in some books.

Related plants: Northern suncup (*Oenothera heterantha*, also called *Camissonia subacaulis*) has large, 4-petaled, yellow flowers that seem to bloom directly from the ground. It is found in grassy areas. Like all members of the evening-primrose family, suncup has an 'inferior' ovary (situated beneath the petals), and since the petals are flat on the ground, the ovary of this flower is actually underground—a convenient location for planting the seeds!

ROCKY SLOPES • RED FLOWERS • 4 PETALS, UNITED IN A TUBE

RANGE: Baja California to southern Oregon; east to Wyoming.
TAHOE LOCATIONS: Frequent on rock ledges from
about 6500' to 8000'.

ROCK FRINGE
Epilobium obcordatum ～ *Evening-primrose Family*

As the common name beautifully implies, this gorgeous flower grows in rocky soil at the edges of boulders, ledges, and cliffs. **The four heart-shaped petals make a luxuriant, deep rose flower that is more than 1" wide**, which is unusually large for the short creeping stems. Rock fringe typically grows in large, low mats that splash the austere rock habitat with great palettes of solid rose color; the flowers are so large, and they are packed so closely together that the foliage is often nearly completely concealed. Rock fringe is well suited to its dry, often unstable environment: its long, hardy roots are able to penetrate deep into rocky soil or into cracks in rock ledges to find water and anchorage.

The genus name *Epilobium* means 'atop the ovary,' in reference to the position of the petals above the ovary. This 'inferior' ovary is a characteristic of the evening-primrose family that distinguishes it from the other common 4-petaled family—the mustards—which have a 'superior' ovary (with the petals situated below the ovary).

Related plants: Another rose-colored evening-primrose that is common in Tahoe is **fireweed** (*E. angustifolium*), whose leaves turn bright scarlet in the fall.

ROCKY FLATS AND SLOPES • RED FLOWERS • 4 SEPARATE PETALS

RANGE: Throughout the western mountains.
TAHOE LOCATIONS: Infrequent around boulders and in scree from about 8200' to 10,000'.

SIERRA PRIMROSE
Primula suffrutescens ⌐ *Primrose Family*

The exquisite, rose-red Sierra primrose is quite uncommon in Tahoe, but when you find it, it will usually be in large masses. It **grows among rocks**, usually on north-facing cliffs where late-melting snow can provide constant moisture. Sierra primrose is a bit more common in the southern Sierra, but, strangely enough, in Tahoe it is only found north of Lake Tahoe.

Though the flowers are not especially large, each 2–5" stem bears several. The resulting carpet of brilliant rose blossoms nearly conceals the wedge-shaped rosettes of toothed, basal leaves. The five petals of each flower are deeply lobed and are united at the base into a 'pinwheel.' The **rich rose** of the petals is contrasted by a **bright yellow center**.

**ROCK LEDGES AND SLOPES • ROSE-COLORED FLOWERS
5 SEPARATE PETALS, UNITED ONLY AT THE BASE**

RANGE: Only in the mountains of California.
TAHOE LOCATIONS: Uncommon under rock overhangs and on rocky cliffs from about 8000' to 10,000'.

MOUNTAIN PRIDE
Penstemon newberryi ~ *Snapdragon Family*

Mountain pride is a frequent and showy flower of rocky slopes. It grows in low, compact masses that typically carpet large areas of rock with nearly solid red, **often resembling a red cascade tumbling down rock slopes**. Like all members of the snapdragon family, its flower is a 2-lipped tube, which in this case is quite large (1–1$^{1}/_{2}$"). The toothed leaves are stiff and leathery, which is a frequent characteristic of dry-environment plants.

As the genus name indicates, penstemons have five stamens. However, one of the stamens is nonfunctional: it has no anther and is therefore sterile.

Related plants: The spectacular deep blue-purple, large-flowered **showy penstemon** (*Penstemon speciosus*) and the smaller-flowered, blue **meadow penstemon** (*P. rydbergii*), which forms immense fields of blue in mid-elevation meadows, are both frequent in Tahoe.

ROCK LEDGES AND CLIFFS • RED FLOWERS
5 PETALS, UNITED IN A 2-LIPPED TUBE

RANGE: Restricted to the mountains of California, western Nevada, and Oregon.
TAHOE LOCATIONS: Common on rocky slopes from about 6400' to 9500'.

One of the late-season flowers of rocky environments, western eupatorium will be found in bloom well into September. Although it is not as striking as some of the other late-blooming, rocky-habitat plants (such as California fuchsia [p. 35] and Sierra primrose [p. 37]), western eupatorium nonetheless provides some dashes of color to a mostly brown fall landscape.

As with other members of the composite (or sunflower) family, the flowerheads consist of many separate flowers that are clustered together to resemble one many-petaled flower. Eupatorium, however, is not as showy as most composites, for it has no ray flowers. Instead, **each white or pink flower head consists of a tight cluster of many long, narrowly tubular disk flowers, from which protrude forked styles.** Close examination of one of these thread-like flowers will reveal five tiny petals joined in a star atop a small tube.

Western eupatorium is given the scientific name *Ageratina occidentalis* in some books.

ROCKY SLOPES AND LEDGES • PINK TO PURPLE TO WHITE FLOWERHEADS • MANY TINY DISK FLOWERS

RANGE: Limited to the mountains of the West (the 'occident').
TAHOE LOCATIONS: Occasional in rocky soil and about rocks from about 6800' to 9700'.

PONDS & SMALL LAKE EDGES

ALTHOUGH THERE ARE MANY WET environments along streams and in soggy meadows in Tahoe (see chapter 4, p. 47), there are only occasional aquatic environments where standing water maintains a fairly stable level throughout the summer. In the shallow edges of small ponds, especially at Yellow Pine and lower Red Fir elevations where ponds are unfrozen for several months during spring and summer, certain plants thrive afloat on pond surfaces.

The aquatic environment may be the most demanding of all; because it requires the most specialized adaptations, few species of plants can survive there. Only a small number of plants are able to flourish in standing water, where obtaining sufficient sunlight and oxygen can be a major problem.

These aquatic plants, which sprout from the muddy pond bottoms, have to grow quickly, so that within a few weeks the stems reach the pond surface, where the leaves and flowers can float. To aid in rapid growth and flotation, the stems are usually hollow. The leaves are usually broad (to aid in flotation and to catch sunlight), and they have their stomata (pores) only on the upper surface, away from the water. Aquatic plants sometimes don't bear blossoms until the second year.

Although most of the plants described here typically grow just at pond edges, in shallow ponds plants like pond-lily may sometimes cover most of the pond surface, concealing the water with a solid mass of leaves and large, bright blossoms.

Blooms living in ponds!—seems remote.
You'd think that they'd need a large boat.
But while roots in muck wallow,
the stems have cores hollow
to raise blossoms and leaves till they float.

DUCK POTATO, ARUM-LEAF ARROWHEAD
Sagittaria cuneata ∾ *Water-plantain Family*

Duck potato is not as flashy as its fellow pond dweller yellow pond-lily (p. 44), but it is nevertheless conspicuous with its **bright white flowers and arrowhead leaves.** It is uncommon in Tahoe, being found occasionally in shallow ponds, where its flower clusters rise 6–12" above the pond surface. Its leaves, atop their own stems, float or hang slightly above the water. The flowers are unisexual (either male or female), and the female flowers are usually lower on the stem than the male flowers. In both male and female flowers, the three white petals surround a central cluster of yellow reproductive parts.

Both the genus name *Sagittaria* (arrow) and species name *cuneata* (wedge-shaped) refer to the distinctive shape of the leaves.

Related plants: Another interesting white flower of ponds (and streams) is **aquatic buttercup** (*Ranunculus aquatilis*), which has five petals and deeply divided, thread-like leaves. This member of the buttercup family sometimes blooms underwater—in the few places it occurs, I've seen it in blossom for most of the blooming season at least 6" under the surface of a creek!

PONDS AND OTHER STANDING WATER
WHITE FLOWERS • 3 SEPARATE PETALS

RANGE: In shallow ponds from California to British Columbia, east to Nova Scotia.
TAHOE LOCATIONS: Uncommon in shallow ponds from lake level to about 7500'.

Buckbean is an uncommon plant of standing water and a very unusual representative of the gentian family (so unusual that some books separate it into its own family—the buckbean family). A stem bearing numerous white flowers rises above the fleshy leaves, which are divided into three leaflets each. The five or six petals of each flower flare out from the flower tube, forming a star. The **petals are covered with dense, thread-like, white hairs** that give the flower a furry, somewhat unkempt appearance. The fleshy, green stigma is 2-parted, and it rises above deep maroon-purple anthers.

The genus name *Menyanthes* means 'month,' in reference to the approximate length of flowering, and the species name *trifoliata* refers to the three leaflets of each leaf. The leaves, by the way, can be used as a hops substitute in beer-making—talk about a medicinal plant!

Related plants: Two other odd-looking flowers of standing water (especially bogs) are the insectivorous **round-leaved sundew** (*Drosera rotundifolia*) and **long-leaved sundew** (*D. anglica*). They have long, red, sticky leaf hairs that trap unlucky insects to be digested by the plant. These fascinating plants can be found in only two or three locations in Tahoe.

STANDING WATER • WHITE FLOWERS
5 PETALS, UNITED IN A TUBE

RANGE: Occasionally in bogs and shallow ponds in western mountains and in Eurasia.

TAHOE LOCATIONS: Uncommon (but in the few places you find it, it will occur in large masses) in the shallows of lakes and ponds at the south end of Tahoe, up to about 9000'.

YELLOW POND-LILY
Nuphar polysepalum ⚭ *Water-lily Family*

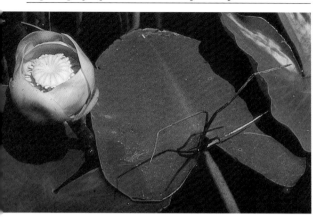

Yellow pond-lily has large, stunning flowers that rise slightly above the surface of quiet ponds on stout, hollow stems. The **bright yellow-orange of this dazzling 1–2" flower** contrasts vividly with the deep green of the large, leathery, heart-shaped leaves that float on the pond surface. Most of the color of the flower comes from the 5 to 14 petal-like sepals that form the flower cup; the 10 to 20 small petals are obscured by the many yellow (sometimes red-tinged) stamens and the large pistil.

It is not easy to have a close look at this gorgeous flower, because the plant **rarely grows in less than 3' of water**. A 'mud-squishy' tiptoe through the muck of the pond bottom might be the price of 'admission' … but the show is spectacular! Pond-lily often occurs in huge masses on quiet ponds, sometimes completely obscuring the water.

Each spring, new leaf stems grow from the rootstock on the pond floor until they reach the surface, where the leaf blade expands and floats. As you would probably expect, the stomata (pores) only occur on the upper surface of the leaves.

**PONDS • YELLOW TO ORANGE FLOWERS
5–14 SEPARATE 'PETALS' (ACTUALLY SEPALS)**

RANGE: California to Alaska; east to the Rockies.
TAHOE LOCATIONS: Common in ponds from about 6200' to 7500'.

PURPLE CINQUEFOIL
Potentilla palustris ∽ *Rose Family*

Just when you are feeling confident that cinquefoils are one flower you really know and can recognize—five uniform, yellow petals surrounding a clump of many reproductive parts on a plant growing in a grassy open area—you find this purple anomaly thriving in a pond, and that confidence is shaken! Purple cinquefoil has the five separate petals and large central cluster of reproductive parts that are typical of cinquefoils (and of the rose family), but its exotic **wine-purple color** and water habitat are most definitely not typical!

Each stalk (up to 2' tall) bears only a few flowers above sharply toothed, pinnately (sometimes palmately) compound leaves.

The species name *palustris* is apt; it indicates this plant's preference for swampy locales.

**STANDING WATER • RED TO PURPLE FLOWERS
5 SEPARATE PETALS**

RANGE: Bogs and lake shallows throughout North America and into Eurasia.
TAHOE LOCATIONS: Uncommon in swamps and shallow ponds, especially in the southern portions of Tahoe, up to about 8000'.

WET MEADOWS, STREAMBANKS, & SEEPS

MANY AREAS FROM LAKE LEVEL up to timberline have abundant water for most of the summer. Damp creek- and streambanks, seeps in rock cracks, and meadows under slopes holding late-lying snow: all these areas provide wet or damp environments, though each has special characteristics that are conducive to somewhat different associations of plants.

The wet environment is in many ways the least severe for plants; there is usually an abundance of moisture, soil, and sunlight. Most plants of this environment are large and robust, with tall stems (frequently over 2' and occasionally over 6'), long, broad leaves, and a profusion of large flowers or large clusters of flowers. In wet or damp meadows it is not unusual to find lush gardens packed with many species of large-leaf plants.

On moist banks along creeks and streams, you will typically find such flowers as Sierra rein orchid, green orchid, elephantheads, Jeffrey's shooting star, tiger lily, brook saxifrage, willowherb, monkshood, larkspur, and Lewis monkeyflower. Many of these plants are found 'cutting across' life zones, from lake level up into Subalpine elevations, but none of them is found away from wet or damp environments. This illustrates that for many wildflowers (unlike trees), the micro-environment of an area is a more important influence than its life zone.

Although some of the same plants that grow on damp streambanks can also be found in moist, grassy meadows, certain plants are much more common in meadows than near running water. Look for the following plants in damp meadows: camas lily, great red paintbrush, dirty socks, fan-leaf cinquefoil, arrowleaf senecio, Jacob's ladder, ranger's buttons, cow parsnip, and Macloskey's violet.

Most rocky slopes and ledges are dry and sparsely soiled, and they support only a few plants specially adapted to those conditions. Some rocky areas have occasional seeps, however, where water and soil accumulate. In addition to mosses, you can expect to find a few wildflowers in these micro-habitats,

notably death camas, explorer's gentian, and several monkeyflowers.

Some meadows lie directly below leeward, shady slopes where snow accumulates to great depth and remains as a constant source of water for all or most of the summer. These meadows, and others with a constant water inflow or poor drainage, are quite soggy much of the time. Especially in late spring or early summer, meadows with so much water will freeze on many nights. Despite this difficult early-season environment, you will find several plants there that typically sprout in May and bloom shortly thereafter. In such spring bogs, look for marsh marigold, water-plantain buttercup, Nevada lewisia, three-leaf lewisia, toad lily, and corn lily (which sprouts early, but doesn't bloom until much later). It is interesting to note that all of these 'coldwater-venturers' (except corn lily) are not the typical large plants of wet environments, but instead are rather small.

There are some areas above timberline that have wet environments, but they are rare, because strong winds blow most of the snow off unprotected alpine slopes and flats, and the intense solar radiation speeds evaporation. The wet environment plants discussed in this chapter therefore seldom occur above timberline.

This wet meadow menagerie ode
is for all those lush creatures there growed:
Cow, Monkey, and Frog
all thrive in the bog
with Elephant, Tiger, and Toad.

Violets are easily recognized by their petal arrangement and backward-extending nectar spur. In Macloskey's violet (**the only all-white violet in the Sierra Nevada**) the two upper petals are slightly bent back, the two side petals are slightly bent down, and the bottom petal is heavily streaked with purple. As in all violets, a short spur extends back from the bottom petal. The solitary flower nods from a short stem that rises above fleshy, round or kidney-shaped basal leaves. Macloskey's violet often grows in clumps, for it has runners that root at the nodes and produce new stems.

As in many violets, Macloskey's violet has an interesting back-up mechanism to pollination to ensure reproduction: late in the summer, if the showy flowers have dried up without being pollinated, the plant produces small, greenish flowers that sit on the ground and pollinate themselves within the closed bud. Self-pollination is not a real good idea—recessive genes can become dominant and there is no expansion of the gene pool—but in dire circumstances it is better than nothing!

WET MEADOWS • WHITE FLOWERS • 5 SEPARATE PETALS

RANGE: Throughout the western mountains and in the northeast United States.
TAHOE LOCATIONS: Occasional in wet meadows from about 6800' to 9000'.

COW PARSNIP
Heracleum lanatum ∞ *Umbel Family*

Probably the largest of the Tahoe flowering plants, cow parsnip is enormous in everything but its flowers, which are tiny. The **thick, hollow stem may grow as tall as 10', the maple-like leaves are 6–16" long and nearly as wide, and the dense, flat heads of tiny, 5-petaled, white flowers are up to 1' across**. The flowers grow on 'umbrella spoke' stalks (pedicels) that all radiate from the same point on the stem. This type of flower cluster, called an umbel, is the distinguishing characteristic of plants in the umbel family (also called the carrot family or parsley family).

The genus name is derived from 'Hercules,' presumably because of the enormous size of the plants of this genus.

Related plants: Other common, white-flowered members of the umbel family include **ranger's buttons** (*Sphenosciadium capitellatum*), which has its flowers clustered in spherical heads; **angelica** (*Angelica breweri*), which has pinnately compound leaves; and **Gray's lovage** (*Ligusticum grayi*), which has deeply divided, lacy leaves.

**WET MEADOWS • WHITE FLOWERS, IN LARGE CLUSTERS
5 TINY PETALS**

RANGE: Widespread across most of North America.
TAHOE LOCATIONS: Common in moist places from lake level to about 8000'.

FRINGED GRASS-OF-PARNASSUS
Parnassia fimbriata ~ *Saxifrage Family*

Fringed grass-of-Parnassus is probably the rarest of the several intriguing members of the saxifrage family in the Tahoe area. The large (1") creamy flowers sit atop 6–20" stems, several of which cluster in each plant. Most of the kidney-shaped leaves are attached to the ends of leaf stems (petioles) that are only about half as long as the stem that bears the solitary flower.

What makes the flower so unusual are the **fringes along the lower edge** of each of the five petals and the **yellow, fan-shaped, knobby-tipped glands** that surround the large pistil.

The genus name refers to Mt. Parnassus, the mythical home of the nine muses of song and poetry; perhaps it is someone's poetic response to the flower's delicate and artistic petal fringes!

WET STREAMBANKS • WHITE FLOWERS • 5 SEPARATE PETALS

RANGE: Mid-elevations in the western mountains, from Placer County in California to Alaska; east to the Rockies.
TAHOE LOCATIONS: Rare in wet streambanks at lower Red Fir elevations, from about 6500' to 8000'.

BREWER'S MITREWORT, BREWER'S BISHOP CAP
Mitella breweri ∽ *Saxifrage Family*

Certainly one of the strangest and most fragile-looking of all Tahoe wildflowers is the tiny mitrewort. Above a cluster of lush, toothed, maple-like basal leaves rises a 4–12" leafless stem that bears several of the tiny flowers spaced along its upper portions. Each flower has five greenish-white petals that form feathery 'antennae' extending beyond the round sepals. **This strange plant looks for all the world like it has tiny spiders clinging to its stem!** Like all members of the saxifrage family, the ovary of a mitrewort flower is split in two, a feature that is much easier to see when the flower is in seed.

This species is named after William Brewer, a Californian botanist and geologist, for whom many Sierra plants are named.

Related plants: Several other saxifrages with delicate white flowers occur in wet environments, including **bog saxifrage** (*Saxifraga oregona*), which has tall fleshy stalks supporting dense clusters of small flowers, and **brook saxifrage** (*S. punctata*), whose small flowers branch individually on delicate, thin, reddish stems.

WET MEADOWS AND STREAMBANKS
WHITE TO GREEN FLOWERS • 5 SEPARATE PETALS

RANGE: The Sierra Nevada to Montana and British Columbia.
TAHOE LOCATIONS: Fairly common in wet meadows and along creekbanks from about 6400' to 9000'.

SIERRA REIN ORCHID
Habenaria dilatata ～ *Orchid Family*

A monocot with long, grass-like leaves, Sierra rein orchid is recognizable as an orchid by its oddly shaped flowers. The upper two petals join with the upper sepal to form a hood-like structure, the two narrow lower sepals stick out to the sides, and the long lower petal hangs straight down, tapering at the lower end. (All orchids have five 'petals' [actually two petals and three sepals] that are more or less alike, and one petal that is often dramatically different.)

The most distinctive feature of Sierra rein orchid is the long, thin spur that curves down from the back of the lower petal. Its resemblance (well, sort of) to a horse's rein is the origin of both the common and genus names. The $^1/_2$" flowers are white and occur along nearly the entire length of the 1–3' spike.

Sierra rein orchid is given the scientific name *Platanthera leucostachys* in some books.

Related plants: A very similar orchid of the same wet environment is **sparsely flowered bog orchid** (*Habenaria sparsiflora*, also called *P. sparsiflora*). Its greenish-white flowers are (as the name suggests) less abundant and less densely packed on the stem than those of Sierra rein orchid.

WET MEADOWS AND STREAMBANKS • WHITE TO GREENISH FLOWERS • 6 SEPARATE 'PETALS' (3 ARE ACTUALLY SEPALS)

RANGE: Across most of North America.
TAHOE LOCATIONS: Common in wet meadows and along creekbanks, from about 7200' to 8300'.

CORN LILY
Veratrum californicum ~ *Lily Family*

When they first appear in early spring, shortly after the snow recedes, corn lily's large, parallel-veined leaves are wrapped in a tight, cigar-like roll from which the tall flower spike will later emerge. By late summer, the plant is 3–5' tall, and its leaves are 6–16" long and 2–6" wide. All this phenomenal growth occurs in just one summer, for although corn lily is a perennial, only the roots persist over the winter.

Corn lily is a striking plant, not just for its size, but also for its **spike of 6-petaled, greenish-white flowers**, which towers above the corn-like leaves. In late summer, a damp meadow that is crowded with densely flowered corn lily stalks is very impressive (and not uncommon, for this plant typically grows in large clumps). In dry years, you may still find many corn lily plants, but no flower stalks.

It is important to be able to identify corn lily, for it is **extremely poisonous**; it paralyzes the respiratory system, reputedly after turning everything green! When corn lily first comes up, hikers sometimes mistake it for the highly edible skunk cabbage, with disastrous (even fatal) results.

**WET MEADOWS • WHITE TO GREENISH FLOWERS
6 SEPARATE 'PETALS' (3 ARE ACTUALLY SEPALS)**

RANGE: Throughout the western mountains.
TAHOE LOCATIONS: Common in wet meadows
from about 6400' to 9500'.

MARSH MARIGOLD
Caltha howellii ~ *Buttercup Family*

When the snow begins to melt off high mountain meadows in the spring—exposing cold, soggy soil—a few plants push up above ground and begin to bloom. One of these early risers is marsh marigold, which sometimes even pushes through thin snow and blooms while its leaves and stems are still snow-covered. In early spring, when most plants have only begun to think about appearing, it is not uncommon to find large parts of wet meadows packed nearly solid with this showy flower.

Marsh marigold is a striking flower: its **large, bright white blossoms**, which sit on 4–12" **naked stems**, contrast sharply with the **large, glossy, fleshy, heart- or kidney-shaped leaves**. The flowers, like those of many members of the buttercup family, do not have a fixed number of 'petals' (actually sepals); there are **usually 5 to 10, but sometimes there are 20 or more**!

Marsh marigold is given the scientific name *Caltha leptosepala* in some books.

Related plants: Another member of the buttercup family that often blooms in great masses with marsh marigold in early spring is **water-plantain buttercup** (*Ranunculus alismaefolius*), a smaller flower with a variable number of glossy yellow petals (actually sepals). During a midnight full-moon hike to a high mountain meadow one early spring, I couldn't believe my eyes when I saw a boggy field full of blooming buttercups sparkling in the moon, each blossom encased in its own miniature block of ice!

**WET MEADOWS • WHITE FLOWERS
5–10 SEPARATE 'PETALS' (ACTUALLY SEPALS)**

RANGE: The central Sierra to the mountains of Alaska.
TAHOE LOCATIONS: Common in soggy meadows from about 6400' to 9200'.

MOUNTAIN CHICKWEED
LONG-STALKED STARWORT
Stellaria longipes ∽ *Pink Family*

Mountain chickweed is a dainty plant that is common in the damp, grassy environments of Tahoe. You will find it partly hidden in the grass, its **small white flowers** nonetheless quite conspicuous for their brightness and their **red anthers**. At first glance you might think that the flower is a 'composite' with many ray flowers, but a closer look will show that there are only five petals, each of which is deeply cleft in two. In addition, the five sepals are nearly as long as the petals and show through the spaces between them. The deep clefting of the petals is characteristic of flowers in the pink (as in 'pinked') family.

This is one of those wildflowers that holds back some of its charms until you put forth the effort to get to know it. You need to lie in the grass and examine it up close (perhaps with a magnifying glass) to fully appreciate its personality and exquisite details. Looking closely at several flowers might puzzle you at first, however, for some appear to have red dots on the petals and others don't. Mountain chickweed flowers (especially their reproductive parts) go through subtle changes as their blooming season progresses. See if you can figure it out.

The genus name *Stellaria* is very descriptive of this chickweed; it often sprinkles grassy meadows with its delicate, white, **star-like flowers**.

DAMP, GRASSY MEADOWS • WHITE FLOWERS
5 SEPARATE PETALS, EACH DEEPLY CLEFT

RANGE: Circumboreal; widespread across North America.
TAHOE LOCATIONS: Common in damp, grassy meadows from lake level to about 8700'.

The **white-to-pink** flower of Nevada lewisia sits atop a stem that grows no taller than 4". The bowl-shaped flower is sometimes partially hidden by the fleshy, linear basal leaves. As in many lewisias, the number of petals is variable (there are **usually 6 petals**, but there may be as many as 10 or 12), which is unusual for a dicot. Nevada lewisia has only **two sepals** (as in all members of the purslane family) that form a pair of green, cradling 'hands' beneath the petals. Just remember: there are two sepals in the purslane family, like the two 'lips' of a purse.

The genus *Lewisia* is named after Meriwether Lewis of the Lewis and Clark Expedition.

Related plants: Several other white-flowered purslanes (all with only two sepals) can be found in Tahoe: **three-leaf lewisia** (*L. triphylla*) has a pair or trio of linear leaves that point straight up from the stem; **toad lily** (*Claytonia chamissoi*, also called *Montia chamissoi*) has small, 5-petaled flowers, and it has red runners connecting plants; **spring beauty** (*C. lanceolata*) has peppermint-striped, white flowers, and it occurs only occasionally in forest openings.

**WET AND DRYING MEADOWS • WHITE FLOWERS
5–10 SEPARATE PETALS**

RANGE: Throughout the western mountains.
TAHOE LOCATIONS: Fairly common in wet and drying meadows up to timberline.

SIERRA CORYDALIS
Corydalis caseana ∽ *Fumitory Family*

An extremely rare flower in Tahoe, but one that grows in great profusion in the few very wet places in which it occurs, is the bizarre and wonderful Sierra corydalis. Corydalis and steershead (p. 31) are both members of the fumitory family (now considered by botanists to be part of the poppy family), but Sierra corydalis is unlike its relative in many ways: it (unlike steershead) is readily noticeable when it blooms, for many of its large tubular, white to pink flowers lie tightly packed atop each other on the tall (to 4') leafy stems. The **spurred, open-mouthed flowers all face in different directions**, as though they are trying to decide which way to go, or perhaps performing 360° sentry duty.

Be sure to get close and smell these blooms, for they exude a delightful, **grape-like fragrance**. This delicious aroma is so strong, however, that you may not need to get close—you'll probably be haunted by a vague 'grape-aciousness' long before you see the flowers!

WET CREEKBANKS • WHITE TO PINK FLOWERS
4 SEPARATE PETALS

RANGE: Uncommon in the mountains of the West.
TAHOE LOCATIONS: Rare, but when you find the right spot, you'll find hundreds of them. Follow your nose and good luck!

ARROWLEAF SENECIO
ARROWLEAF GROUNDSEL
Senecio triangularis ∽ Sunflower Family

There are so many different kinds of yellow, sunflower-like composite flowers, that you might decide to just call them all 'yellow sunflowers.' Many of these similar flowers can be readily distinguished, however, if you know what to look for. Arrowleaf senecio is one of the easiest of these plants to identify, because the flowerheads and especially the leaves are quite distinctive. The flowerheads have five to eight narrow, **widely separated rays** (each of which is actually an individual flower with its own reproductive parts) and many disk flowers. Six to 12 flowerheads grow close together at the ends of very tall (to 6') stems. Senecio flowerheads always appear somewhat scraggly, because their ray flowers are fewer and more separated than in most composites: it

almost looks like someone has eaten some of the rays. Senecios are also identified by the black dots at the tips of the phyllaries (the narrow, green bracts under the flowerhead). This particular senecio is characterized, as the name suggests, by its **large, arrowhead-like leaves**, which are broad at the base and taper to a sharp point.

The genus name *Senecio* is related to our word 'senile,' and it refers to the white pappus (hair) at the tops of the seeds—not that white hair implies senility! Senecios are also called 'groundsels,' meaning 'ground-swallowing,' in reference to their tendency to take over large areas.

WET, GRASSY MEADOWS • YELLOW FLOWERHEADS
SEVERAL RAY FLOWERS AND MANY DISK FLOWERS

RANGE: Common throughout the western mountains.
TAHOE LOCATIONS: Very common in wet meadows from lake level to about 9000'.

TIGER LILY, ALPINE LILY
Lilium parvum ∽ Lily Family

Most wildflowers are dicotyledons, meaning that they have two tiny leaves (cotyledons) in their embryo form. When you see a flower that appears to have three or six petals and grass-like leaves, you can be sure it is a monocotyledon (having only one embryonic leaf). This knowledge is a great help in plant identification—I know you're wondering how … who's going to go poking around embryos?—because there aren't many families or genera of monocots (other than the grasses, sedges, and such). The only non-grass monocot families in Tahoe are the lily, orchid, iris, and amaryllis (which includes onions and brodaieas) families.

Tiger lily is a typical member of the lily family. It has six identical petals that form a large, open, showy flower. Three of the 'petals' are actually sepals that have evolved to look like petals, making the flower even more alluring to insects. The leaves, which (on all but the upper parts of the stem) whorl around the stem, are somewhat broader than grass leaves. Everything about this plant is on a grand scale: as many as 40 flowers may branch off this tall (up to 6') plant!

The **bright orange petals with maroon spots**—I thought tigers had stripes!—make tiger lily stand out dramatically, even from the dense tangle of willows and alders among which it usually grows.

**WET MEADOWS AND STREAMBANKS • ORANGE FLOWERS
6 SEPARATE 'PETALS' (3 ARE ACTUALLY SEPALS)**

RANGE: Only in the Sierra Nevada.
TAHOE LOCATIONS: Occasional in wet meadows and streambanks from lake level to about 8000'.

Elephants in Tahoe!? Not only that, but herds of **pink** elephants! Like steershead (p. 31), this flower is an amazing 'totem' that bears an uncanny resemblance to its mammalian namesake. As in all members of the snapdragon family, the flowers form **2-lipped tubes**. In elephantheads, the two petals of the upper lip unite to form the long, upcurving '**trunk**,' while the outer two petals of the lower lip form large, flaring '**elephant ears**.' The third petal of the lower lip forms the '**head**.'

The arrangement of the flowers on the stalk make this plant even more striking: the 1–2' stalks, which rise above the fern-like basal leaves, are densely covered with a herd of the $^1/_2$", pink-to-lavender flowers.

Related plants: Little elephantheads (*Pedicularis attolens*) is quite similar, except that the flowers have 'trunks' that curve down, sickle-like, from the upper lip. The two species of elephantheads often grow together, and the same species of bee pollinates both of them indiscriminately. The elephantheads maintain their species integrity by the different positions of the 'trunks': a bee picks up pollen on its forehead from *P. atollens*, and on its chest from *P. groenlandica*—quite an experience, I'm sure!

**WET MEADOWS AND STREAMBANKS • PINK TO PURPLE FLOWERS
5 PETALS, UNITED IN A 2-LIPPED TUBE**

RANGE: Across most of northern, western, and eastern North America (but despite its name, not in Greenland).

TAHOE LOCATIONS: Fairly common in wet meadows and creekbanks from lake level to about 8400'.

LEWIS MONKEYFLOWER
Mimulus lewisii ∽ *Snapdragon Family*

Lewis monkeyflower is the largest monkeyflower in Tahoe, and it is one of the showiest of all Tahoe flowers. It has **large, flaring petals of deep pink**. Toward the throat of the flower tube there are **white patches** that have several **bright yellow, hairy ridges** running through them. These ridges are the nectar guides … the landing strips … the 'Eat-at-Joe's' signs! Several flowers branch from each 1–3' stem, and since the plants usually grow in large clusters, the overall effect is a dazzling sea of dozens of eager pink faces peering out of a jungle of large, lush leaves.

On almost any warm summer day, you can sit by a cluster of Lewis monkeyflowers and watch the hummingbird-like sphinx moth dart from flower to flower, sipping nectar and seemingly not missing a single blossom.

Related plants: You will find many other monkeyflowers in Tahoe, including several large yellow ones, many red ones (p. 83) and a small yellow one—**primrose monkeyflower** (*Mimulus primuloides*)—that grows close to the ground above silky-haired leaves, which usually hold drops of moisture.

**WET MEADOWS AND STREAMBANKS • PINK FLOWERS
5 PETALS, UNITED IN A 2-LIPPED TUBE**

RANGE: Throughout the western mountains.
TAHOE LOCATIONS: Common in wet meadows and streambanks from lake level to about 9000'.

JEFFREY'S SHOOTING STAR
Dodecatheon jeffreyi ☞ *Primrose Family*

With its petals sharply bent back to expose the 'nose' of pistil and stamens, the ½–1" flower of a Jeffrey's shooting star can indeed remind you of its heavenly namesake. The effect is enhanced by the position of the flower on the plant: it hangs upside-down from the end of a tall, branched, leafless stem that rises considerably above the oval basal leaves. The color of the flower is quite striking as well, for the petals are an **intense rose pink**, with **bands of white and bright yellow** at their base. Immediately below these bands is the dark purple of the flower's 'nose.'

These inside-out flowers bloom in early summer in soggy meadows, raising their noses to the sky after being pollinated, as though soaring back to the heavens in jubilation. You—and the bees—can always tell who has and who hasn't!

In late summer, the petals fall off and the green sepals, which were previously hidden by the reflexed petals, fold up to form a protective shell for the exposed seed capsule. The seed capsule is an artistic and engineering marvel: hundreds of small, polygonal seeds fit together like fastidiously and precisely laid Turkish tiles.

WET MEADOWS AND STREAMBANKS • PINK FLOWERS
4 PETALS (RARELY 5), UNITED AT THEIR BASE

RANGE: Southern Sierra to Alaska; east to Montana.
TAHOE LOCATIONS: Common in wet meadows and along streams from about 6500' to 8800'.

NAKED BROOMRAPE
Orobanche uniflora ☞ Broomrape Family

Naked broomrape is a small parasitic plant that can occasionally be found in damp-to-wet soil in Tahoe. Each plant has only a **single flower** and **no leaves**. The flower grows close to the ground on a short (to 2"), naked (leafless) stem, and it looks like a penstemon flower (pp. 38 & 129). It is usually **pink or purplish**, or sometimes **yellow**. The tubular flower and the short, narrow stem are fringed with fine white hairs.

The somewhat brutal genus name—it means 'vetch strangler'—and the common name 'broomrape' refer to this plant's parasitic habit. (Vetches and brooms are the plants that some broomrapes parasitize.) The species name *uniflora* means, appropriately, 'single flower.'

Related plants: Another broomrape that you might find in dry, sandy soil is **clustered broomrape** (*Orobanche fasciculata*), which has many yellow flowers in a cluster of stems on the same plant.

**DAMP GRASSY AREAS • PINK, PURPLE, OR YELLOW FLOWERS
5 PETALS, UNITED IN A 2-LIPPED TUBE**

RANGE: Throughout the mountains of the West and in eastern North America.
TAHOE LOCATIONS: Uncommon in damp areas from about 6400' to 8500'.

CAMAS LILY
Camassia quamash ~ *Lily Family*

It's early spring, and you are out exploring low-lying boggy meadows. Up on the slopes above, you see still-heavy snow glistening in the sun; off in the distance across the meadow you see a dark blue lake shimmering in the warm breeze—at least you think it's a lake.

The **deep blue** petals (and sepals) of camas lily, which are narrow and widely separated, form a 1–2", star-shaped flower, and several flowers branch off each 1–3' stem. Camas lilies usually grow in huge masses, sometimes acres; from a distance they look for all the world like a lake!

This spectacular flower is color-coded for the beginning botanist: ovary green; anthers yellow; petals and sepals blue (or purple). As in most lilies, the three sepals have adapted to look almost exactly like the three petals, producing a showy bloom that attracts a lot of attention from pollinators and human appreciators alike.

Camas lily bulbs were a major food source for Native Americans, and the genus name, derived from the Northwest Native American name for this plant, means 'sweet.'

Related plants: Death camas (*Zigadenus venenosus*) sometimes grows with camas lily, and it has caused bulb gatherers (including several members of the Lewis and Clark Expedition) great problems. The flowers of these two lilies are vastly different (death camas flowers are small, white, and densely clustered on the stem), but the bulbs are almost identical, except that death camas bulbs are as deadly as the name suggests!

**WET MEADOWS • BLUE-PURPLE FLOWERS
6 SEPARATE 'PETALS' (3 ARE ACTUALLY SEPALS)**

RANGE: The Sierra Nevada to northwestern Canada.
TAHOE LOCATIONS: Common in wet meadows from lake level to about 7500'.

65

IDAHO BLUE-EYED GRASS
Sisyrinchium idahoense ∼ *Iris Family*

Although it often hides among tall blades of grass, Idaho blue-eyed grass nonetheless has very striking flowers (if you can find them). One or a few of the rich blue or purple flowers sit atop an unbranched, 6–24" stem. Each flower has six intense blue-purple 'petals' (three of which are actually sepals that are adapted to look like petals) with darker purple veins and spiked tips. The flower's most distinctive feature, however, is the **bright yellow splotch** at the base of each petal. Nectar gland, right? That's apparently what insects think too, but they're in for a real disappointment when they crawl onto the flower tube looking for nectar—they pollinate the flower in the process, of course—because it's a fake; this flower has no nectar. I guess blue-eyed grass hopes that the bees will keep their disappointment to themselves!

The leaves of Idaho blue-eyed grass are typical of monocots: broad, flat, and grass-like. Although you might think blue-eyed grass is a lily from its characteristics, it is actually in the iris family.

**WET, GRASSY MEADOWS • BLUE OR PURPLE FLOWERS
6 SEPARATE 'PETALS' (3 ARE ACTUALLY SEPALS)**

RANGE: The Sierra Nevada to Washington and Idaho.
TAHOE LOCATIONS: Occasional in wet, grassy meadows from lake level to about 8200'.

ALPINE VERONICA, ALPINE SPEEDWELL
Veronica alpina ∽ *Snapdragon Family*

In a land of unparalleled blues—from the early spring 'lakes' of camas lilies to Lake Tahoe itself—the delicate yet intense blue of alpine veronica rates right up there with the best. The **four petals** of the tiny flowers are **blue-violet**, with darker **purple streaks**. Use a magnifying glass and its blue world will invite you in for a dip.

Although it is not immediately obvious, the flower is a 2-lipped tube—characteristic of the snapdragon family. The upper lip consists of one large, rounded petal (formed by the fusion of the two upper-lip petals), while the lower lip has three narrower petals. The reproductive parts are quite unusual: there are **only two stamens**, which protrude with the pistil from the flower cup. Several of the small flowers cluster loosely together at the tip of the slender, hairy, 4–12" stem. Along this stem are four to seven pairs of small, oval leaves.

Alpine veronica is given the scientific name *Veronica wormskjoldii* in some books.

Related plants: You may find **brooklime** (*V. americana*) along streams at lower elevations. It is a larger, coarser plant with similar flowers.

**WET MEADOWS AND STREAMBANKS • BLUE FLOWERS
4 PETALS, UNITED IN A 2-LIPPED TUBE**

RANGE: Throughout the western mountains.
TAHOE LOCATIONS: Common in wet meadows and streambanks from about 7200' to 9000'.

EXPLORER'S GENTIAN
Gentiana calycosa ∽ Gentian Family

In very late summer and fall, only a few species of flowers are in bloom. Happily, they are among the most beautiful and showiest. In September, what the flaming scarlet trumpets of California fuchsia (p. 35) are to dry, rocky areas, so the deep-blue funnels of explorer's gentian are to the damp margins of creeks and rock walls.

Each short stem has a few **large tubular flowers** above a profusion of dark green, oval leaves. A close-up look at the flower reveals a great delicacy: sky-blue petals liberally sprinkled with **tiny, pale greenish spots**, slender **fringes** between the petals, and sensual **dark-purple sepals**.

I spent one crisp fall afternoon watching a large bumblebee crawl deep into one gentian flower tube after another. It plunged headfirst into delight; then it shakily backed out drunk with pollen and nectar.

Related plants: Another blue-flowered gentian is **hiker's gentian** (*Gentiana simplex*, also called *Gentianopsis simplex*). It is found only rarely in Tahoe, and it has smaller flowers with more-flared, fringed petals that are twisted so that they overlap each other in a pinwheel-like arrangement.

**DAMP CREEKBANKS AND SEEPS • BLUE FLOWERS
5 PETALS, UNITED IN A TUBE**

RANGE: Throughout the western mountains.
TAHOE LOCATIONS: Occasional along creeks and in seep areas in rocks, from about 7000' to 9800'.

JACOB'S LADDER, GREAT POLEMONIUM
Polemonium caeruleum ↝ Phlox Family

Polemonium flowers have five petals united into a bowl (or a tube), long, protruding reproductive parts, and a 3-cleft style, all of which are typical of the phlox family. The fact that polemoniums grow in wet environments is very atypical, however, since almost all other members of the phlox family grow on dry flats and slopes (and have narrow, needle-like leaves to reduce evaporation).

Jacob's ladder leaves have as many as **30 leaflets** arranged **pinnately** on each leaf stalk (like the rungs of a ladder). Many of the lovely, pale blue flowers branch off the upper part of the 1–3' tall stem.

Jacob's ladder is especially interesting to revisit through the blooming season. Early on, the stamens are brash and ripe, while the pistil is hidden and closed; later, the pistil is open and receptive, but the stamens are all dried up! This is one of the fascinating mechanisms flowers use to reduce the chances of self-pollination.

Jacob's ladder is given the scientific name *Polemonium occidentale* in some books.

Related plants: There are two other polemoniums in Tahoe that have very similar flowers but different habitats and growth forms: **low polemonium** (*P. californicum*) brings lovely blues to mid-elevation forest openings; **showy polemonium** (*P. pulcherrimum*) does the same for rocky areas near and above timberline.

**WET, GRASSY MEADOWS • BLUE FLOWERS
5 PETALS, UNITED IN A BOWL**

RANGE: Throughout the western mountains.
TAHOE LOCATIONS: Common in wet meadows from lake level to about 8500'.

MONKSHOOD
Aconitum columbianum ∽ *Buttercup Family*

Monkshood, a member of the extremely variable buttercup family, is easily recognized by its oddly shaped blossom. The **large blue-purple flower consists of five sepals: the upper sepal forms the hood** (or cowl) that gives monkshood its name; the two side sepals cup together to form the bulk of the flower; and the two small, narrow lower sepals hang down at the base of the flower. There are only two true petals; they are blue or whitish, tiny, and hidden with the nectaries under the hood.

Monkshood is a large plant—it grows up to 6' tall—and there are many flowers branching off the stout stem. Monkshood is pollinated exclusively by just one species of bumblebee whose size, weight, and tongue length are a perfect match for the flower. Early settlers from Europe brought monkshood with them to America, but didn't bring the bee. Oops! The plant just wouldn't pollinate. The bumblebee soon got an invitation to come over too!

Related plants: Another member of the buttercup family with oddly shaped, blue flowers is **larkspur** (*Delphinium* sp.). Its flowers have long nectar spurs, and its dolphin-like flower buds 'swim' through the air.

**WET, GRASSY MEADOWS • BLUE-PURPLE FLOWERS
5 SEPARATE 'PETALS' (ACTUALLY SEPALS)**

RANGE: Throughout the western mountains.
TAHOE LOCATIONS: Occasional in wet meadows and streambanks from lake level to about 8700'.

Porterella carnosula ∼ *Bellflower Family*

One of the happiest-looking Tahoe wildflowers (and quite uncommon) is the blue-purple, yellow, and white porterella, which grows in the highly specialized environment of **drying vernal pools**. As small spring ponds dry out with the advance of summer, the caked mud that was the pond bottom sprouts a few species of plants, the most colorful of which is porterella.

Its 2-lipped flower tubes (quite similar to those of the snapdragon family) sport **five blue to purple petals**. The lower three petals are marked with **bright yellow 'eyes' on white splotches**. The plant stems are short and tightly clustered, resulting in wonderfully dense mats of intense and joyful colors. What appears to be part of the flower stem is actually the **inferior ovary**, which will swell with the developing seeds after pollination. Porterella is one of the few annuals in Tahoe.

Related plants: Another blue-purple, yellow and white annual of the bellflower family is **Bacigalupi's downingia** (*Downingia bacigalupii*). It is even rarer in Tahoe, and its upper two petals are separated into two 'horns.'

**DRYING POND BOTTOMS • BLUE TO PURPLE FLOWERS
5 PETALS, UNITED IN A 2-LIPPED TUBE**

RANGES: In drying vernal pools throughout the western mountains.
TAHOE LOCATIONS: Uncommon in drying vernal pools
up to about 8000'.

DRY, OPEN
SLOPES & FLATS

IN MOST YEARS THERE IS very little summer precipitation in the Tahoe Sierra, so many of the slopes and flats that are away from streams are exceedingly dry. Whether because of soil that is too poor and dry to support forests, or because of logging or fire, there are often dry, nearly treeless slopes that support a great variety of plants especially suited to such a dry, exposed environment. This is particularly true of south-facing slopes, which are exposed to direct sun year-round.

With even a brief walk across a dry slope in Tahoe (or a quick look at the photographs in this section), you will notice certain similarities among dry-environment plants, and differences between these plants and those of wet environments. Notice especially the leaves—the main point of contact between plants and their environments. While the leaves of most wet-environment plants are large and thin, with only a few exceptions (such as mule ears), the leaves of dry-environment plants are small and narrow, thereby presenting less surface area from which water can evaporate. In addition, the leaves of many dry-environment plants are thick and leathery, and they may be waxy to the touch. Some dry-environment plants also have hairy leaves, which retain dew and reflect light.

Though plants of dry areas are often widely spaced, some dry-slope gardens are surprisingly thick and colorful, indicating remarkably successful plant adaptation to these severe conditions. The dense thickets of chaparral (evergreen shrubs adapted to heat and fire) found especially on south-facing slopes are one striking example of such adaptation.

Though sun-beaten slopes short on moisture
would not for my home be first choice, you're
ambushed by Thistle
and can't wet your whistle,
but somehow tough plants can rejoice here.

LEICHTLIN'S MARIPOSA LILY
Calochortus leichtlinii ∼ *Lily Family*

Leichtlin's mariposa lily is one of the few lilies of dry environments, but it is common and widespread. It is also spectacular: its **three large, bright white petals** form a broad, shallow **bowl**; at the base of each petal is a **hairy, yellow nectar gland** with a **dark red, maroon, or black spot** just above it. Plants frequently have just a single flower, but sometimes as many as 9 or 10 flowers sit atop the 6–24" stem. Leichtlin's mariposa lily usually grows in large clusters, so it presents a brilliant show in this often austere, dry environment. As with nearly all monocots, mariposa lilies have grass-like leaves. The leaves may be overlooked, however, since they shrivel early in the blooming season—a very effective way of reducing evaporation.

The genus name *Calochortus* means 'beautiful grass.' The common name 'mariposa' means 'butterfly,' in reference to the gorgeous 'wings' of the showy flower.

DRY FLATS • WHITE FLOWERS • 3 SEPARATE PETALS

RANGE: Limited to the Sierra Nevada and to the mountains of western Nevada.
TAHOE LOCATIONS: Common on dry, sandy, or gravelly slopes from lake level to about 9700'.

PRETTY FACE, GOLDEN BRODIAEA
Brodiaea lutea ~ *Amaryllis Family*

Pretty face is easily identified as a monocot by its six petals (three of which are actually sepals) and grass-like leaves. It is easily recognized as a member of the amaryllis family by its umbel flower clusters, in which numerous flower stems radiate like umbrella spokes from the same spot on the plant stem.

Pretty face is almost startling in its beauty: each **large (at least ¹/₂") golden petal** (and sepal) has a **dark purple midvein** extending nearly to its tip. The midveins are just as prominent when the flower is in bud. Each plant has several flowers poised delicately at the ends of upsweeping stalks. Pretty face tends to grow in large patches, covering great areas of dry ground with smiling, pretty 'faces.' The long, grass-like leaves are few, and they can be missed easily, since they dry up in early summer.

Pretty face is given the scientific name *Triteleia ixioides* in some books. Botanists have recently moved the entire amaryllis family into the lily family.

Related plants: The only white brodiaea in Tahoe, **hyacinth brodiaea** (*Brodiaea hyacintha*, also called *T. hyacintha*), has more subtle beauty. It is more frequently found in the Sierra Nevada foothills.

DRY FLATS • YELLOW FLOWERS
6 SEPARATE 'PETALS' (3 ARE ACTUALLY SEPALS)

RANGE: California and southern Oregon.
TAHOE LOCATIONS: Common on open, dry flats from lake level to about 9000'.

WOODY-FRUITED EVENING-PRIMROSE
Oenothera xylocarpa ➤ Evening-primrose Family

Size, color, fragrance, rarity: woody-fruited evening-primrose has it all! Spectacular!

The large (2–3"), **bright yellow flowers** consist of four papery, notched petals that are separate to the base. The petals overlap to form a shallow bowl from which a sticky, 4-parted stigma protrudes. As with other evening-primroses, the flowers are most open in the late afternoon and evening, and they close by mid-morning.

The brilliant petals contrast sharply with the sandy soil and the red-spotted, gray-green leaves on which they nearly rest. The most amazing contrast, however, is between the **sun yellow of the fresh blossoms and the deep scarlet of the dried blossoms**, which remain intact on the plant. You might be so dazzled by the sight of this plant that you don't even think to smell it. Do!

DRY, SANDY SLOPES • YELLOW FLOWERS • 4 SEPARATE PETALS

RANGE: The Sierra Nevada and in the Great Basin.
TAHOE LOCATIONS: Rare on dry, sandy slopes of Mt. Rose only (in the northeastern part of the Tahoe Basin), from about 9000' to 10,000'.

Mule ears is common in Tahoe, often **covering entire hillsides** with its large yellow flowers and gray-green leaves.

Each 1–3' plant stem bears one or a few **3", bright yellow composite flowers**, each of which consists of 5 to 10 long rays and a yellow-brown central disk. Since its flowerheads are so large, mule ears is perfect for understanding the structure of composites; you can easily see the white, feathery pistil attached to each ray flower and the reproductive parts that protrude from the tubular disk flowers. Truly, these flowers are 'composites' of many flowers (probably more than 100), and if only one flower (ray or disk) is pollinated, the entire plant can reproduce.

As large as the flowers are, the leaves are probably this plant's most conspicuous feature. Unlike most dry-environment plants, mule ears has very large leaves. To partly compensate for the evaporation disadvantage this great surface area presents, the leaves are covered with silky, white hairs (*mollis* means 'soft'), and they are oriented vertically (to reduce their exposure to the sun).

Related plants: A very similar yellow composite that often grows with mule ears (and is easily confused with it) is **balsamroot** (*Balsamorhiza sagittata*), which is distinguishable by its arrow-shaped, bright green leaves and its somewhat earlier blooming time.

**DRY SLOPES • YELLOW FLOWERHEADS
MANY RAY AND DISK FLOWERS**

RANGE: The Sierra Nevada to Oregon.
TAHOE LOCATIONS: Very common, often covering dry hillsides from lake level to about 8500'.

DOUGLAS WALLFLOWER
Erysimum perenne ∽ *Mustard Family*

Atop the single, unbranched stem of Douglas wallflower is a large, round-topped cluster of many **bright yellow** (sometimes orange) flowers. Like all mustards, Douglas wallflower has **four separate petals** that form a cross and very distinctive seed pods. After the petals drop off, the 2–4" long, narrow, flattened seed pods develop. The narrow leaves occur mostly at the base of the stem, but they also alternate part-way up toward the flower cluster.

The genus name *Erysimum* means 'help,' in reference to the medicinal properties of many *Erysimum* species. Be sure to smell the flower; it's good medicine indeed! Douglas wallflower is given the scientific name *E. capitatum* ssp. *perenne* in some books.

Related plants: There are many mustards in Tahoe, including the white-flowered, aquatic **watercress** (*Rorippa nasturtium-aquaticum*), which can almost completely choke narrow streams—the botanical name alone might choke a stream!—and the uncommon, pink-to-purple **dagger pod** (*Phoenicaulis cheiranthoides*), which grows on rocky ledges.

DRY, GRAVELLY SLOPES
YELLOW (SOMETIMES ORANGE) FLOWERS • 4 SEPARATE PETALS

RANGE: California and Nevada; north to Oregon.
TAHOE LOCATIONS: Common on dry, gravelly slopes from lake level to above timberline.

Agastache urticifolia ∽ *Mint Family*

Horse-mint is a typical mint: it has a **square stem, a mint aroma, and 2-lipped, tubular flowers**. It is a large, coarse plant that has many **broad, toothed, triangular leaves in opposite pairs** along the 3–5' tall stems. Dense clusters of rose-lavender or white flowers are packed into a long, terminal flower spike. Many horse-mint plants usually grow together in dense 'forests,' which illustrates the genus name *Agastache*, meaning 'many spikes.' Two pairs of stamens protrude from each flower, giving the flower spike a soft, fuzzy appearance.

Related plants: Another very common mint of Tahoe-area dry slopes is **pennyroyal** (*Monardella odoratissima*). Its white, pink or lavender flowers, which are in spherical heads, are incredibly *odoratissima* (aromatic). You always know when you're walking through pennyroyal even if you don't see it. Its 'flavor' is so strong that you can make a tea by swirling a flower or a leaf in cold water. Drink pennyroyal tea in moderation—Native Americans used it as an intestinal cleanser and even, in high doses, as an abortive.

**DRY FLATS AND SLOPES • PINK TO WHITE FLOWERS
5 PETALS, UNITED IN A 2-LIPPED TUBE**

RANGE: Throughout the mountains of the West.
TAHOE LOCATIONS: Common in dry meadows and rocky flats from lake level to about 9000'.

WHISKER BRUSH
Linanthus ciliatus ∽ *Phlox Family*

   The common name of this annual plant is quite descriptive, for
clumps of **prickly, white-hairy, needle-like leaflets**—each clump
does indeed resemble a **shaving brush** (or so I've been told, since
I'm not on intimate terms with that item myself!)—are spaced every
inch or so along the plant's stiff, 4–12" stalk. The small flower tubes
protrude from the uppermost cluster of leaflets. A close look at the
flowers with a magnifying glass reveals an intricate, delicate beauty
that is just implied at first glance: the **five pink-rose petals** flare out of
a **soft yellow flower tube**; and at the base of each petal, at the border
of the yellow and pink, there is a dark, rose-purple spot or triangle.
   Related plants: Another showy phlox of dry slopes is **great
collomia** (*Collomia grandiflora*). It is a large plant that has clusters
of salmon-colored, trumpet-like flowers.

**DRY FLATS AND SLOPES • PINK FLOWERS
5 PETALS, UNITED IN A FLARING TUBE**

RANGE: In the mountains from southern California to Oregon.
TAHOE LOCATIONS: Common on dry flats and slopes from lake level
to about 8500'.

Gilia leptalea ⌒ *Phlox Family*

With its short slender stems, small narrow leaves, and small flowers, Bridge's gilia would be easy to overlook if it weren't so colorful and didn't grow in such masses. If you see a **pale pink-purple carpet** delicately coloring a dry, sandy flat or forest opening, it is very likely to be this wonderful phlox. Bridge's gilia's colorful protruding anthers, small tubular flowers, and needle-like leaves are typical of the phlox family.

The flower consists of a short, narrow tube that rises from the tiny green sepals and flares into five star-like, pink or lavender petals. The inside of the flower tube (this is another magnifying-glass flower … come to think of it, every flower is a magnifying-glass flower!) may be the same exquisite pink or lavender as the petals, or it may be a sharply contrasting yellow or white. For an added touch, the long, protruding anthers are often dark blue.

**DRY FLATS AND FOREST OPENINGS • PINK-LAVENDER FLOWERS
5 PETALS, UNITED IN A TUBE**

RANGE: California to southern Oregon.
TAHOE LOCATIONS: Common in large mats in forest openings and dry flats from lake level to about 9000'.

COPELAND'S OWLSCLOVER
Orthocarpus copelandii ❧ *Snapdragon Family*

Copeland's owlsclover **resembles a small paintbrush** (pp. 106 & 107); it has a thick, dense spike of broad, leaf-like bracts on the upper half of its 4–16" stem. Since these bracts, like those of paintbrushes, are colored at the tips (in Copeland's owlsclover they are pink), you might think they are the flower petals. The actual flow–ers, however, are narrow, 2-lipped tubes that peek out from under the bracts (vaguely like owls peering out from a branch). The tip of the whitish flower tube is also pink. The flowers can afford to be inconspicuous since the upper bracts have adapted to look like, and perform the function of, petals—attracting the pollinators.

Copeland's owlsclover is given the scientific name *Orthocarpus cuspidatus* ssp. *copelandii* in some books.

Related plants: Hairy owlsclover (*O. hispidus*)—it is considered a paintbrush (*Castilleja tenuis*) in some books—is much smaller and grows in grassy fields. The lower lip of the tiny flower is formed by yellow, sac-like petals; the upper lip is a narrow beak.

DRY FLATS • PINK FLOWERS
5 PETALS, UNITED IN A 2-LIPPED TUBE

RANGE: Only in dry areas of northern and eastern California and southern Oregon.
TAHOE LOCATIONS: Occasional on dry slopes in the northern parts of Tahoe, from about 6800' to 9000'.

TORREY'S MONKEYFLOWER
Mimulus torreyi ∽ *Snapdragon Family*

Although 'monkeyflower' brings to mind images of bright yellow flowers or large pink flowers cavorting in wet meadows, there are several species that flourish on dry flats or slopes in Tahoe. One such dry-environment monkeyflower is the showy Torrey's monkeyflower, which often covers large areas of dry hillsides with a **low, graceful carpet of pink**. The pink petals flare out of a white flower tube that has yellow ridges; the tiny 1–6" stems also bear small oval leaves.

A fascinating characteristic of all monkeyflowers is the hinged stigma. It closes instantly if it is touched, but it will stay closed only if it was 'correctly' pollinated. If the touch left no pollen (playful botanists?) or if it left the wrong pollen (including pollen from the same plant, which would lead to a genetic clone), the stigma will reopen in a few minutes, ready for another try.

Related plants: Another pink-to-rose monkeyflower of dry flats is the tiny **Brewer's monkeyflower** (*Mimulus breweri*). Its flowers are only ¹/₈" across, but they nonetheless carpet large areas with their soft pink tint.

**DRY FLATS • PINK-ROSE FLOWERS
5 PETALS, UNITED IN A 2-LIPPED TUBE**

RANGE: Only in the Sierra Nevada and in southern Oregon, down to about 1500'.
TAHOE LOCATIONS: Common on dry slopes from lake level up to about 7000'.

SIERRA ONION
Allium campanulatum ⌁ *Amaryllis Family*

   Sierra onion is one of several wild onions that you will find only on hot, dry, open slopes in Tahoe. Many of its small flowers radiate on short pedicels from the top of the plant's slender, 6–12" stem. Each flower has six narrow, pointed 'petals' (three of which are actually sepals) that form a **delicate, rose star.** Each 'petal' is rose at the tip and whitish at the base. **Darker rose streaks and nectar glands** add further decoration. Nectar can often be seen glistening on the petals, and in the warmth of midday you can smell a distinct, though mild, onion aroma. Botanists have recently moved the entire amaryllis family into the lily family.

   Related plants: Dry slopes in Tahoe are also home to the purple, star-flowered **broad-leaf onion** (*Allium platycaule*) and the white (with red-purple markings) **Sierra red onion** (*A. obtusum*), whose flowers lie directly on the ground or on very short stems. In boggy areas, you will occasionally see—and smell—the giant, purple-flowered **swamp onion** (*A. validum*).

**DRY FLATS AND SLOPES • PINK TO ROSE FLOWERS
6 SEPARATE 'PETALS' (3 ARE ACTUALLY SEPALS)**

RANGE: The Sierra Nevada to southern Oregon.
TAHOE LOCATIONS: Common on dry, open slopes from lake level to about 9000'.

LARGE-FLOWERED STEPHANOMERIA
Stephanomeria lactucina ∽ *Sunflower Family*

Now this is some dandelion! Stephanomeria is one of the most beautiful and most unusually colored of the many composites found in Tahoe. The **notched, pink-rose ray flowers**, which have **dark rose veins**, flare gracefully from the top of 4–12" stems, which also bear linear, alternate leaves. There are no disk flowers, but the long, slender styles of the ray flowers protrude from the center of the flowerhead, perhaps giving you (only at first glance, of course!) the impression of many delicate, tubular disk flowers.

Related plants: Another unusually colored composite that only has ray flowers is **orange mountain dandelion** (*Agoseris aurantiaca*). It can be found (rarely) in dry, grassy parts of Tahoe.

**DRY SANDY OR GRAVELLY FLATS • PINK-ROSE FLOWERHEADS
MANY RAY FLOWERS**

RANGE: The mountains from California to southern Oregon.
TAHOE LOCATIONS: Uncommon on sandy or gravelly, dry flats from lake level to about 8000'.

CHECKERMALLOW, GLAUCOUS SIDALCEA
Sidalcea glaucescens ∾ *Mallow Family*

Checkermallow is very common on dry slopes, often sharing volcanic hillsides with fields of mule ears (p. 77). The five separate, pink petals (each of which is distinctively white-veined) overlap to form a deep cup that is 1" or so across. Characteristic of the mallow family, **the male and female parts of each flower occur on the same structure**: the white male parts occur near the base of the column, and the sinuous, thread-like, scarlet female parts grow out of the tip. Inspect several flowers and look for subtle differences in these male and female parts; see if you can figure out the sequence of events in the blooming cycle.

The hollyhock-like leaves have five to seven lobes. Leaves near the base of the 6–18" stem have broad, shallowly cut lobes, while those higher up the stem have deeply cut, finger-like lobes.

Related plants: You will also find **marsh mallow** (*Sidalcea oregona*) in wet areas. Its flowers look very much like those of checkermallow, but they are smaller and several grow on each flower spike.

DRY FLATS AND SLOPES • PINK FLOWERS • 5 SEPARATE PETALS

RANGE: Only in the Sierra Nevada and in the mountains of western Nevada and southern Oregon.
TAHOE LOCATIONS: Very common on dry slopes from lake level to about 9500'.

Cirsium andersonii ∽ *Sunflower Family*

Because thistles spread rapidly, choke out other plants, and frequently grow in disturbed areas, some people think of them as undesirable weeds. But perhaps 'weed' is all in the eye of the beholder. Anderson's thistle's 1–3' stalk bears many bright red flowerheads, which attract all sorts of hummingbirds, to say nothing of wildflower lovers.

The flowerheads of this composite consist of hundreds of tubular disk flowers, each of which produces a large amount of readily available nectar. The stems are covered with woolly hairs that apparently discourage ants ('poor' pollinators with limited range) from reaching the nectar, which is then available for the far more mobile hummingbirds. If you want to be buzzed by these guided missiles, sit among Anderson's thistle at dusk (and wear a pith helmet!).

Related plants: In higher elevations, you may find **Drummond's thistle** (*Cirsium drummondii*, also called *C. scariosum*), which has creamy white flowerheads that bloom squat in a rosette of prickly leaves. It is one of the few stemless members of this genus.

DRY FLATS • PINK TO ROSE FLOWERHEADS
MANY SPINY DISK FLOWERS

RANGE: The Sierra Nevada and east to Nevada and Idaho.
TAHOE LOCATIONS: Common on dry slopes and in disturbed areas from lake level to about 9000'.

SCARLET GILIA
Ipomopsis aggregata ⮞ *Phlox Family*

Scarlet gilia is certainly one of the most spectacular of our dry-environment flowers: great masses of its **bright red trumpets** adorn large areas of dry, sandy (often volcanic) slopes. The 2–3' stems typically have only a few narrow leaves, but they display many of the dazzling flowers, whose scarlet petal lobes flare out in a star shape from their narrow tubes. Occasionally, you will find pale pink or even white flowers.

Scarlet gilia is a biennial; the first year of growth produces only a rosette of basal leaves; the flower stalk and blossoms don't appear until the second year, after which the plant dies.

The genus name *Ipomopsis* was well chosen indeed; it means 'striking appearance'!

Related plants: At elevations near and above timberline, you may find **ballhead gilia** (*I. congesta*), which has dense spherical heads of small, tubular, white-to-lavender flowers.

**DRY FLATS AND SLOPES • RED FLOWERS
5 PETALS, UNITED IN A TUBE**

RANGE: The mountains from southern California to Oregon, and in the Rockies.
TAHOE LOCATIONS: Common on dry, sandy slopes from lake level to about 9000'.

Dwarf waterleaf is one of those plants whose leaves are more distinctive and more noticeable than its flowers. The leaves are large, soft-hairy, and deeply lobed. Each leaf grows on its own nearly erect, 4–10" stem. The flowers sit atop separate stems that grow only 1" or so above the ground, so they are **almost completely hidden beneath the leaves**. If you part the leaves, however, you will find that dwarf waterleaf has delicately beautiful, blue-purple flowers. Like almost all flowers of the waterleaf family, they have long, protruding stamens, which create the characteristic fuzzy appearance.

Related plants: California waterleaf (*Hydrophyllum occidentale*) is similar, but its clusters of blue flowers rise above the leaves on long stalks. It is found in forest clearings in Tahoe.

DRY FLATS • BLUE-PURPLE FLOWERS
5 PETALS, UNITED IN A TUBE

RANGE: Northern California to Oregon; east to Idaho.
TAHOE LOCATIONS: Common in open, dryish areas (often among sagebrush) from lake level to about 9700'.

LOW PHACELIA
Phacelia humilis ⁓ *Waterleaf Family*

The ground-hugging low phacelia carpets **large areas of dry, sandy flats** with an intense, joyful **purple or violet**. The stems of this dwarfed annual plant are only 2–8" tall, but the flowers grow in dense coils on the stems and many plants grow together; the result is a canvas of vibrant color amid often drab surroundings. Each flower is a small, 5-petaled bowl that cradles several protruding stamens, producing the somewhat fuzzy appearance typical of this family. The leaves, which are oblong and rather hairy, sometimes partially conceal the flower clusters.

The Latin nomenclature is certainly appropriate and descriptive: the species name *humilis* means 'low-growing,' and the genus name *Phacelia* means 'clustered.'

**DRY FLATS • BLUE, PURPLE, OR VIOLET FLOWERS
5 PETALS, UNITED IN A BOWL**

RANGE: The Sierra Nevada (mostly along its eastern edge) to eastern Washington.
TAHOE LOCATIONS: Fairly common on dry flats from lake level to about 8500'.

Each tall, slender stem of blue flax bears many narrow leaves and several of the large, **steely blue flowers**, whose five broad petals are separate to the base, but overlap to form a shallow bowl. The flowers are delicate not only in color but in construction as well, so be gentle—if you inadvertently brush a stem as you pass, you will probably dislodge several petals. Each flower only blooms for a short time, but there are so many flowers on each plant that a field of blue flax will be in bloom for several weeks.

To reduce the chances of a plant self-pollinating, blue flax has two different types of flowers, which never occur on the same plant. In one flower type, the style is long and the filaments are short; in the other, the style is short and the filaments are long. A flower with a short style can be pollinated only from a flower with short filaments (which occurs only on a different plant) and vice versa.

The genus name *Linum* means 'thread'; it refers to the tough, fibrous stems, which in some species are the source of commercial flax. Western blue flax is given the scientific name *L. lewisii* in some books.

DRY, SANDY FLATS • BLUE FLOWERS • 5 SEPARATE PETALS

RANGE: Widespread throughout the western mountains from Mexico to Alaska.
TAHOE LOCATIONS: Occasional on dry, sandy slopes from lake level to about 9000'.

VELVETY STICKSEED, VELVETY FORGET-ME-NOT
Hackelia velutina ∽ *Borage Family*

Despite its striking, **blue or pink flowers**, velvety stickseed is probably best known and most easily identified by its **prickly seeds**. A late-summer or fall walk through grassy or shrubby slopes will likely result in quite a collection of burrs and barbed seeds on your socks and legs, and chances are good that many of these will be the green, round, barbed seeds of velvety stickseed.

Velvety stickseed has narrow leaves and many $1/2$" flowers along the 1–2' stem. Each flower has five petals, which are united at the base into a small tube. In most plants, the buds are pink and the flowers are blue, but sometimes the petals remain pink well into the blooming season.

As the common name and the species name *velutina* suggest, the leaves are covered with soft, white hairs.

Related plants: Another common stickseed with much smaller flowers is **Jessica's stickseed** (*Hackelia jessica*, also called *H. micrantha*). It also grows in dry areas, sometimes together with velvety stickseed.

**DRY FLATS AND SLOPES • BLUE FLOWERS
5 PETALS, UNITED IN A BOWL**

RANGE: Common, but limited to California and Oregon.
TAHOE LOCATIONS: Very common on dry slopes from lake level to about 9000'.

Joining several other striking violets in Tahoe is the 2-toned Beckwith violet, an immigrant from the 'deserts' to the east. It is one of the first flowers to bloom in dry environments—a welcome sight in the spring. The flowers and the gray-green leaves grow on separate stems, none of which exceed 9–10", though the flowers rise slightly above the surrounding leaves.

The **upper two petals are a rich, velvety maroon**, while the **lower three petals are a deep red-purple** (or rarely white). The bases of the lower petals are yellow, with purple veins running through them. (Colored veins on the lower petals, especially the middle one, is typical of violets.) Unlike many of the violets, Beckwith violet does not produce any second, 'backup' flowers.

Related plants: There are several yellow violets that grow in dry environments in Tahoe, including **mountain violet** (*Viola purpurea*) which, as its species name suggests, has a brownish-purple backing to its two upper petals. Two interesting blue violets of wet areas are **bog violet** (*V. nephrophylla*, also called *V. sororia*), which has its flowers and leaves on separate stems, and **long-spurred violet** (*V. adunca*), which has its leaves and flowers on the same stems.

DRY FLATS • PURPLE TO MAROON FLOWERS
5 SEPARATE PETALS, WITH A NECTAR SPUR

RANGE: The eastern parts of California and Oregon, and in the cold, high deserts of Idaho, Utah, and Nevada.
TAHOE LOCATIONS: Uncommon, though locally profuse, in dry areas to the north and east of Lake Tahoe, at around lake level.

SQUAW CARPET
Ceanothus prostratus ∽ *Buckthorn Family*

Squaw carpet is typical of the buckthorn family with its **dense clusters of small, fragrant flowers**, but it is **unusual for its ground-hugging growth form and its blue blossoms**. The stems trail on the ground and root frequently, creating leaf mats that are only a few inches high but many feet long and wide.

The leaves are very attractive: they are thick and waxy, wedge-shaped (like holly) and toothed at the tip. When the plant is in bloom, the leaves are covered by masses of the blue flowers; when the plant is in seed, the bright red berries nearly conceal the leaves.

Many people want to transplant squaw carpet for a garden ground cover, but it loves its wild environment and strongly resists being moved!

Related plants: All members of the buckthorn family (also called the California lilac family) are considered part of the chaparral community, which is made up of evergreen shrubs that are highly adapted to heat and fire—are in fact dependent on them for long-term survival. Chaparral plants like the prickly **whitethorn** (*Ceanothus cordulatus*) and the often red-barked **greenleaf manzanita** (*Arctostaphylos patula*, a member of the heath family) need intense heat to germinate their seeds, and they will quickly resprout from rootcrowns after fires. **Tobacco brush** (*C. velutinus*) even aids and abets fires with its highly flammable, oil-laden leaves, thereby killing off competing plants that cannot return so quickly after being burned.

**DRY FLATS AND SLOPES • BLUE FLOWERS
5 SMALL, SEPARATE PETALS**

RANGE: California and western Nevada to Washington.
TAHOE LOCATIONS: Common on dry slopes from lake level to about 7800'.

PURPLE NIGHTSHADE
Solanum xantii ∞ *Nightshade Family*

Purple nightshade is a beautiful but rather ominous-looking, **purple-violet, bowl-shaped flower** that bears a **yellow 'corncob'** in its center and a disquieting name. Each sticky, 1–2' stem bears 6 to 10 of the large, shallow flowers, whose five united petals are the texture of crinkled crepe paper. Of sharp contrast to the vivid purple of the petals are the large, bright yellow anthers, which unite to form that 'corncob' projecting out of the bowl. When the plant goes to seed, it has round, light green berries.

The ominous name and appearance of this plant serve as appropriate warnings: purple nightshade contains a poisonous narcotic that can be fatal.

**DRY FLATS • BLUE TO PURPLE FLOWERS
5 PETALS, UNITED IN A SHALLOW BOWL**

RANGE: Only in the Sierra Nevada and the desert mountains of southern California and Baja.
TAHOE LOCATIONS: Uncommon on dry slopes, especially along trails and roadcuts from lake level to about 8000'.

GRASSY MEADOWS & OTHER DAMP-TO-DRYISH AREAS

THE ENVIRONMENTS DESCRIBED IN THIS book so far—deep forests, rocky ledges and slopes, standing water, wet meadows and streambanks, dry slopes—all present extreme conditions to plant life. Although many different plants grow in these environments, the plants of any one environmental type tend to be similar in many aspects, since the severity or extremity of the environment requires special plant adaptations for survival. For example, many plants of deep shade are parasitic or saprophytic, and have no green leaves, while most plants of dry environments have small, narrow leaves for reduced evaporation. Wet environments are extreme, but not usually severe; they don't require special plant characteristics other than the robustness to compete with all the other plants of that environment.

Not all environments in Tahoe present such extreme conditions. There are many places where the soil is not especially rocky or shady or bright-sunny or wet or parched, but only slightly damp or dryish. These damp-to-dryish, open slopes harbor many varied plants that are not suited to survival in more severe or extreme environments.

Moderate environments may be the result of partial shade, north-facing slopes, proximity (but not too much so) to creeks or seeps, or late-summer drying of previously wet meadows. You can find many examples of this environment at various elevations: open subalpine meadows, shrubby slopes near seeps, dryish edges of damp meadows, openings in forests, or meadows drying with the advancing season. Some of Tahoe's most colorful and profusely growing flowers inhabit these 'neither here nor there,' damp-to-dry environments.

Though shunning sites arid or oozy,
these plants aren't especially choosy.
They'll happily encamp
in spots dryish or damp,
and live in bright sun or shade snoozy.

WOODLAND STAR, ROCK STAR
Lithophragma glabrum ∾ *Saxifrage Family*

Woodland star is a lovely, delicate flower of forest clearings and open meadows. Although its **deeply cleft petals** would seem to put it in the pink family, close inspection—very close inspection—will reveal the **2-beaked style** characteristic of the saxifrage family. This feature is much easier to see when the plant is in seed.

Each slender stem bears several loosely arranged, white or pink flowers and a few small leaves. Most of the plant's leaves are basal, as in many of the saxifrages, but both the basal leaves and the stem leaves are, like the petals, deeply cleft into three or five lobes. Late in the blooming cycle, you may find tiny red globules attached to the stem; these 'bulbils' will later fall off the plant and sprout—an interesting, nonsexual, backup method of reproduction.

FOREST CLEARINGS AND OPEN MEADOWS
WHITE OR PINK FLOWERS • 5 SEPARATE, 3-CLEFT PETALS

RANGE: The Sierra Nevada to Colorado and British Columbia.
TAHOE LOCATIONS: Occasional in forest clearings and open meadows from lake level to about 9500'.

ALPINE GENTIAN
Gentiana newberryi ~ *Gentian Family*

Although alpine gentian has a large, white, tubular flower that is conspicuously marked with greenish spots, this plant is not easy to find because it grows so low to the ground that it is often hidden by the surrounding grass. The stems are decumbent, rarely lifting the flower more than 1–2" off the ground. When you do locate this gentian, you will see that it is of uncommon beauty: the white tube is not only **speckled with greenish spots**, but it is marked by **vertical, purplish bands**, it has **short fringes** between the five petals, and it is often **tinged bluish**. The 1–2" leaves are fleshy and spatulate.

Related plants: Another striking member of the gentian family is **deer's tongue** (*Frasera speciosa*, also called *Swertia radiata*). It is found in dry areas at the south end of Lake Tahoe, and it has an enormous 6' stalk with multitudes of spectacular, 4-petaled, greenish-white, mottled flowers. It would be hard to be much more different from alpine gentian or explorer's gentian (p. 68) and still be in the same family!

GRASSY MEADOWS • WHITE FLOWERS
5 PETALS, UNITED IN A TUBE

RANGE: The Sierra Nevada to southern Oregon.
TAHOE LOCATIONS: Uncommon in open, grassy meadows at high elevations, from about 7000' to 9000'.

WASHINGTON LILY
Lilium washingtonianum ∽ *Lily Family*

   Washington lily is the **largest and certainly one of the showiest members of a very showy family**: it has as many as 20 very large (3–4"), trumpet-shaped, white blossoms on each 3–8' plant. The gorgeous flowers are softly fragrant and tend to turn pink with age. The light green, oval leaves occur in several whorls along the stem.

   One disadvantage of being so spectacular is that unaware or uncaring people tend to pick you. Washington lily (the epitome of an 'Easter lily') is found only occasionally these days in Tahoe. If you are fortunate enough to come upon one of these beauties, please leave it where it is and smile in the knowledge that the next person to see this sensational flower will share the pleasure.

   The species name was given to this plant in 1863 in honor of Martha Washington.

FOREST OPENINGS AND BRUSHY SLOPES • WHITE FLOWERS
6 SEPARATE 'PETALS' (3 ARE ACTUALLY SEPALS)

RANGE: Only in the Sierra Nevada and in Oregon; more commonly north of Tahoe in the Sierra Buttes area.
TAHOE LOCATIONS: Uncommon in damp-to-dryish forest openings and on brushy slopes, from lake level to about 7500'.

Although it has the bowl-shaped flower that is typical of the waterleaf family, dwarf hesperochiron is an unusual waterleaf in several ways: its flowers do not have the characteristic fuzzy appearance, nor do they have the 'standard' five petals—they frequently have six petals, or occasionally more.

The **large white flowers** nestle among the **basal rosette of oblong leaves**, for there is no plant stem—the short flower stems rise directly from the leaf axils. Each flower is richly colored with **fine purple veins** and a **deep yellow center**.

Not only is dwarf hesperochiron unusual for its family, but it is also unusual for Tahoe—it is found in only three or four sites.

Related plants: Another intriguing waterleaf, found in damp or dried pond bottoms, is the annual **mitten-leaf nemophila** (*Nemophila spatulata*). It has tiny white flowers that often have purple spots at the tip of each of their five petals, and its leaves do indeed look like mittens … for **very** small people.

**DAMP FOREST CLEARINGS • WHITE FLOWERS
5 OR 6 PETALS, UNITED IN A BOWL**

RANGE: Southern California and Arizona to Washington, and east to Utah and Montana.
TAHOE LOCATIONS: Rare in damp clearings of Red Fir forests, from about 6500' to 7500'.

MOUNTAIN RED ELDERBERRY
Sambucus microbotrys ~ *Honeysuckle Family*

Mountain red elderberry is a low shrub that is easily identifiable by its **conspicuous clusters of white flowers**, which become **bright red berries** in the fall. The 5-petaled (sometimes 4-petaled) flowers are tiny, but they occur in large bunches, and this shrub often grows in dense thickets, so it is not unusual to see great cascades of these flowers 'flowing' along meadow edges or down slopes.

Although mountain red elderberry is a member of the mostly fragrant honeysuckle family, the most noticeable odor of this plant comes from its leaves—an unforgettable and some say pleasant (if you happen to like the smell of **stale peanut butter**!) scent.

The genus name *Sambucus* is from the Greek name for a musical instrument that was made from elderberry wood. Mountain red elderberry is given the scientific name *S. racemosa* var. *microbotrys* in some books.

Related plants: Other shrubs of the honeysuckle family include **twinberry** (*Lonicera involucrata*), which has twin, maroon, 'throne-like' flowers, and **snowberry** (*Symphoricarpos vaccinioides*, also called *S. rotundifolius*), which has creamy white, pasty berries.

**OPEN HILLSIDES AND ROCKY SLOPES • WHITE FLOWERS
5 TINY PETALS**

RANGE: The Sierra Nevada, Oregon, and the Rockies.
TAHOE LOCATIONS: Fairly common in moist to dry meadow edges and rocky slopes from about 6800' to 9700'.

A showy plant with loose clusters of cheerful, **bright yellow flowers**, St. John's wort may initially look like a member of the rose family: its $1/2$" flowers have five uniform, separate petals and a large clump of many long stamens. Unlike the rose family, however, St. John's wort (which has a family all to itself) has **pairs of opposite leaves** along its slender 6–24" stems. The leaves are often speckled with black dots along their edges. In addition, close examination of the mass of stamens will show that they are actually grouped into three **separate clumps**.

For centuries, Europeans hung some species of this plant in their houses in the belief that they would keep away evil.

Related plants: Another member of the St. John's wort family is **tinker's penny** (*Hypericum anagalloides*). It has quite a different growth form and appearance; it carpets wet areas in mats of beautiful, small, orange flowers.

BRUSHY MEADOWS • YELLOW FLOWERS • 5 SEPARATE PETALS

RANGE: California to British Columbia, and in the Rockies.
TAHOE LOCATIONS: Occasional in damp or dry meadows and on shrubby banks from lake level to about 7500'.

SOFT ARNICA
Arnica mollis ∽ *Sunflower Family*

Soft arnica is one of the most beautiful and striking of the many yellow composites in Tahoe, primarily because of its bright color and its tendency to **grow in great masses** (it has underground runners that sprout many stems). You will often see large fields filled almost entirely of arnicas, their 1–2" yellow heads seeming to float atop the hairy 1-2' stems like a meadow-full of suns come to earth.

Each flowerhead is composed of 12 to 18 **bright yellow ray flowers** and a raised dome of **orangish-yellow disk flowers.** The bright flowerheads contrast with the **soft gray-green** of the **two to four pairs of opposite stem leaves,** which are egg-shaped, smooth-edged, and stemless. 'Pairs of opposite leaves' is a key characteristic for Tahoe wildflower enthusiasts who are struggling to distinguish one DYC (damned yellow composite) from another; this trait pretty much guarantees an arnica.

Related plants: Another gorgeous arnica, which usually grows in smaller masses than soft arnica, is **heart-leaf arnica** (*Arnica cordifolia*). Its heart-shaped, paired, opposite leaves announce its presence (and identity) in forest openings.

**GRASSY MEADOWS • YELLOW FLOWERHEADS
MANY RAY AND DISK FLOWERS**

RANGE: The Sierra Nevada to Canada, and in the Rockies.
LOCATIONS: Fairly common in dampish grassy meadows from about 6800' to 9700'.

PURPLE FRITILLARY
SPOTTED MOUNTAIN BELLS
Fritillaria atropurpurea ∽ *Lily Family*

Among the many rewards of spending years roaming an area, getting to know all its moods and intricacies, is that just when it all seems cozy and familiar, you come across a stranger, an unexpected and unknown creature. The 'normal' purple fritillary is relatively uncommon in Tahoe, but it can occasionally be found on dry flats and slopes. The incredible and stunning creature described and illustrated here appears to be a once-in-a-lifetime variation (or perhaps a strange hybrid with Davidson's fritillary [*Fritillaria pinetorum*]).

The usual purple fritillary is beautiful enough (with its ¼–½", widely separated, yellow and maroon mottled 'petals'), but this 'stranger' is something else altogether! It resembles a **bizarre starfish with its six 'arms' fused into a large (to 2") mottled bowl of brown-purple and yellow**. Its amazing corolla/calyx palette is accentuated with brown-purple anthers and a thick, 3-cleft, yellow style.

This strange fritillary has characteristics of Davidson's fritillary (such as the broader, less separated 'petals') and of purple fritillary (such as its nodding flowers), but its nearly completely fused petals are unlike either of them. I saw this beautiful stranger only once—one flower that I have never been able to re-find—on a dry, open slope of Mt. Rose.

DRYISH OPEN SLOPES • YELLOW AND PURPLE MOTTLED FLOWERS • 6 SEPARATE 'PETALS' (3 ARE ACTUALLY SEPALS)

RANGE: The usual purple fritillary occurs in the western mountains from New Mexico to Oregon.
TAHOE LOCATIONS: The usual purple fritillary occurs occasionally on dry slopes from lake level to about 9000'.

PINK PAINTBRUSH
Castilleja pilosa ∾ *Snapdragon Family*

Pink paintbrush is one of the least common of the many paintbrushes in Tahoe; it is also one of the most unusually and exquisitely colored. As with all paintbrushes, the 2-lipped, tubular flowers are almost completely concealed by the colorful, leaf-like bracts. In most paintbrushes these bracts are bright red, orange, or even yellow, but in pink paintbrush they are a much softer, **pastel pink to magenta**. Pink paintbrush usually grows 6–15" tall, in several clumps from the same root crown.

To me, paintbrushes are a gift of perspective, for they shift my perception from snapshots to movies (usually time-lapse). When I see the green leaves at the bottom of the plant slowly change to colored, petal-like bracts toward the top of the plant, I can visualize the slow changing of the leaves over the centuries as they began to mimic petals to attract pollinators, resulting in the atrophying of the actual petals (since they were no longer needed) and the plant's shift to partial parasitism (to compensate for fewer functional leaves). Although we usually think of a flower as a frozen snapshot (in full bloom), it is, of course, a process continually in flux—budding, blooming, seeding, wintering, sprouting—and, on a larger timescale, in continual (though extremely slow) dynamic interplay and adaptation to its environment.

**GRASSY MEADOWS • PINK TO MAGENTA FLOWERS
5 PETALS, IN A 2-LIPPED TUBE**

RANGE: The eastern Sierra Nevada to western Washington.
TAHOE LOCATIONS: Uncommon in grassy meadows at the north end of Tahoe.

Although paintbrushes are members of the snapdragon family, and so have their petals united in 2-lipped tubes, this is not even close to being readily apparent at first glance. The brightly colored parts of a paintbrush are not the petals, but rather the leaf-like bracts below the flowers. The actual flowers have pale greenish-yellow petals and lie concealed between the bracts. The upper two petals are united into a 'beak,' and the lower three petals are reduced to small green, globular bumps. This is a case where you have to adopt 'botanical faith'; you are told that the paintbrush is a member of the snapdragon family, with the typical 2-lipped tubular flower comprised of two petals up and three petals down … yeah, right!

Great red paintbrush is one of the few Tahoe paintbrushes that is red and tall (2–3'), and it is the only one with **smooth-edged, unlobed leaves**. As with all paintbrushes, great red paintbrush is partially parasitic to compensate for the reduced photosynthetic ability that comes from some of its leaves thinking they are petals.

Related plants: The most common paintbrush in Tahoe is the orangish (sometimes quite red) **Applegate's paintbrush** (*Castilleja applegatei*). It is found in dry areas and it has wavy-edged and lobed leaves.

**OPEN GRASSY MEADOWS • RED FLOWERS
5 PETALS, IN A 2-LIPPED TUBE**

RANGE: Throughout the western mountains.
TAHOE LOCATIONS: Common in damp grassy meadows from lake level to about 9000'.

RED HEATHER, MOUNTAIN HEATHER
Phyllodoce breweri ∽ Heath Family

Flowing carpets of the pink to rose red heather are soft and lovely. These low shrubs, which bear **dense clusters of pendant, 5-petaled, cup-like flowers**, are usually found growing profusely in rather damp, acidic soil, such as around mountain lakes, where snow remains well into summer. The graceful, pink flowers have long, protruding stamens whose anthers have small 'pores' from which the pollen is shaken when the anthers are 'triggered' ... hopefully by pollinators. The leaves of this low-growing shrub are thick, needle-like, and evergreen.

Related plants: Other members of the heath family (usually evergreen shrubs with urn-shaped flowers) that you are likely to encounter in Tahoe include the delightful **alpine heather** (*Cassiope mertensiana*) with its pendant, dancing, white bells adorned with deep red sepals, **bog laurel** (*Kalmia polifolia*) with its upright, pale rose flowers hugging the ground, and various species of **huckleberries** (*Vaccinium* spp.) with their urn-shaped, white or pink flowers and delicious berries.

**OPEN AREAS AROUND LAKES • PINK TO ROSE FLOWERS
5 PETALS, UNITED IN A BOWL**

RANGE: The mountains of the central Sierra Nevada to Mt. Lassen.
TAHOE LOCATIONS: Occasional in damp, sometimes rocky areas, often around lakes, from about 6400' to 10,000'.

Among the many fragrant Tahoe wildflowers, mountain rose has **one of the most powerful and delicious aromas**: the pastel hue clings to your nose and caresses your skin.

Very unlike its domestic cousin, the flower of mountain rose has only five petals (slightly overlapping to form a pinwheel), it is comparatively small (1–1¹/₂" across), and it has a central cluster of numerous yellow stamens and pistils. This 3–9' shrub presents quite an offering: rich green, toothed leaves, rather weak thorns, and **many** stunning, fragrant flowers.

Related plants: Other fragrant or tasty members of the rose family that are common in Tahoe include **California strawberry** (*Fragaria californica*), which has white flowers and scrumptious berries, **spiraea** (*Spiraea densiflora*), whose reproductive parts are so thick that you can barely see the small pink petals beneath the dense, pink fuzz, and **thimbleberry** (*Rubus parviflorus*), which has large, white (sometimes pink) flowers and red, raspberry-like (perhaps a bit drier) fruit.

**SHRUBBY SLOPES AND LEDGES • ROSE-COLORED FLOWERS
5 SEPARATE PETALS**

RANGE: The Sierra Nevada to Canada; east to the Rockies.
TAHOE LOCATIONS: Fairly common on open slopes, ledges, and banks from lake level to about 8000'.

DOWNY AVENS, OLD MAN'S WHISKERS
Geum canescens ∼ *Rose Family*

In a family of flowers with interesting fruits (see p. 109), downy avens is no exception. Although its white flowers are very attractive, this plant is most striking and beautiful when it is in seed. The reddish styles are thin and feathery, and they grow long and wavy, producing a dense head of soft, twisting tentacles that is as dramatic as it is delicate (and which leads some to call this plant 'old man's whiskers'). Avens flowers are typical of the rose family, with five separate petals and a clump of many stamens and pistils (though in an avens, **the petals fold up in a puckered 'kiss'**).

The rose family is one of the oldest families of terrestrial flowering plants with the 'remains' of a primal reproduction strategy: lots of males produce lots of pollen and have lots of females to receive it.

Downy avens is given the scientific name *Geum triflorum* in some books.

**GRASSY SLOPES • PINK-RED TO WHITE FLOWERS
5 SEPARATE PETALS**

RANGE: The mountains of northern and eastern California and western Nevada, and in northeastern North America.
TAHOE LOCATIONS: Uncommon on grassy slopes from about 8500' to 10,000'.

Scarlet is right! A stunning plant in many ways, scarlet fritillary bears **many large, hanging, bell-shaped, red flowers from its 2–3' stem**. Each lily flower has yellow mottling on the insides of its six showy, scarlet petals/sepals, which are bent back at their tips and are sometimes purple-tinged on the outside. The six thick anthers are yellow; the protruding style is 3-cleft and is rich scarlet, even deeper red than the petals. The stem also bears two or three **whorls of long, grass-like leaves.**

**FOREST OPENINGS AND GRASSY MEADOWS • RED FLOWERS
6 SEPARATE 'PETALS' (3 ARE ACTUALLY SEPALS)**

RANGE: The Sierra Nevada to southern Oregon, usually at foothill elevations of 3000' to about 6000'.
TAHOE LOCATIONS: Occasional only in forest openings at lake level.

WESTERN PEONY
Paeonia brownii ↝ *Peony Family*

Talk about going to seed; none of us have anything on the peony! **The two to five pistils swell incredibly into fleshy, greenish sausage pods up to 2–3" long**. Each pod houses only a few large, shiny, black seeds. Before the flower goes to seed, the pistils are surrounded by many **bright yellow stamens**, which contrast sharply with the **five or six separate, leathery, maroonish petals**, which overlap to form a cup.

Although the western peony is unusual and showy whether it is in bloom or in seed, it is easily overlooked because the flowers hang close to the ground and are mostly concealed by the large, bluish-green, irregularly lobed leaves. When the plant goes to seed, the stem bends even closer to the ground under the weight of the enormous seed pods.

Western peony resembles a buttercup in structure, with its variable number of petals and clump of many reproductive parts, but botanists have split it off from the buttercups into its own (peony) family.

GRASSY, DRYISH FLATS • MAROON TO BROWN FLOWERS
5 OR 6 SEPARATE PETALS

RANGE: Grassy areas of the mountains from California to British Columbia, and east to Wyoming.
TAHOE LOCATIONS: Common in grassy and dryish areas from lake level to about 8600'.

As a typical member of the mint family, self-heal has a square stem, a mint aroma, and 2-lipped tubular flowers whose lower middle petal is much larger than the other petals—it is a 'landing pad' for pollinators. The upper lip of the flower tube forms a sort of cowl or hanging awning over the long, protruding reproductive parts.

The violet of the petals contrasts lusciously with the reddish-purple sepals. The flowers are tightly packed in a **pinecone-like spike** atop a bright green, square, 4–20" stem, which also bears **pairs of opposite, oblong leaves**, the highest pair of which nestles directly beneath the spike.

There is something about this flower's intense color and intricate form that invites you in. The common name 'self-heal,' in reference to the plant's many medicinal properties, conveys the same feeling.

Related plants: Another intriguing (and uncommon) member of the mint family is the annual **blue curls** (*Trichostema oblonga*), which has small, deeply blue flowers and a powerful camphor-like odor. It is occasionally found in Tahoe in the drying edges of meadows and ponds at around lake level.

**GRASSY MEADOWS • BLUE TO VIOLET FLOWERS
5 PETALS, UNITED IN A 2-LIPPED TUBE**

RANGE: Circumboreal; widespread on both the west and east coasts of North America and across much of the Northern Hemisphere.
TAHOE LOCATIONS: Uncommon in shady, grassy areas from lake level to about 7000'.

ALPINE SLOPES, RIDGES, & PEAKS

AS YOU CLIMB TOWARD THE summits of some of Tahoe's highest peaks, the trees begin to thin out and to take on a battered and embattled appearance. You are approaching timberline, that elevation above which trees cannot grow. At this elevation, wind blasts across exposed ridges and sweeps the ground clear of potentially moisture-giving snow. Solar radiation is intense, but the temperatures are usually low. This cold and the resulting short growing season (perhaps only a month at the very highest elevations) are the main factors determining timberline: there is not enough total heat to enable the production of a tree's extensive woody tissue.

In the Tahoe area, true 'climatic' timberline occurs at about 10,500', near the summits of only the four highest peaks: Freel Peak (10,881'), Job's Sister Peak (10,823'), Job's Peak (10,633'), and Mt. Rose (10,778'). However, on exposed ridges at or near the summits of several lower peaks, the cold wind and poor, rocky soil create a 'pseudo-alpine' environment in which only alpine plants can survive.

What adaptations allow a plant to survive in a world of cold, wind, brief summer, arid soil, and intense solar radiation?

Of course, almost all alpine plants are perennials, which means less time, energy, and materials are required for new plant growth each year, since the roots (and sometimes the stems) remain from year to year.

There are many internal physiological adaptations to cope with the harsh environment (such as an increased ability to respire and photosynthesize at low temperatures), but there are also many external morphological adaptations that help create the powerful beauty of alpine plants.

Probably the most noticeable of these visible adaptations is short stature. Alpine plants rarely have stems more than 1–2" tall, and they often rise only barely above the basal leaves. This dwarf growth form has obvious advantages: there is less plant material to produce; it keeps the plant close to heat radiating from the ground; there are shorter distances to pump water from the roots; and it provides some degree of sanctuary from the cold, drying, tearing wind (taller alpine plants grow almost exclusively behind the shelter of rocks).

In addition to their short stems, alpine plants usually have basal leaves that are often in dense mats or cushions, sometimes so dense that it is difficult to penetrate them with your finger. Besides affording protection from the drying wind, these cushions can create a micro-environment of their own with nighttime temperatures as much as 20° F warmer inside the cushion than outside.

The leaves of alpine plants are typically very small and narrow, which reduces evaporation and tearing by presenting little surface area to the wind. A few alpine plants have thick or leathery leaves, which also minimizes evaporation.

Most alpine plants are covered with white or silvery hairs. It is thought that these hairs serve several purposes: they reflect light, which helps protect the underlying plant from the intense solar radiation and ultraviolet rays that are only slightly filtered by the clear, thin alpine air; they trap dew and other occasional moisture; they protect the plant from the evaporating effects of wind by creating wind 'eddies'; and they provide some insulation from the cold.

Although the prototypical alpine environment is the cold, windswept ridge and summit, it must be remembered that there are occasional micro-environments above timberline that are not typically alpine, such as behind the shelter of a rock or along a spring or melting snowfield. At high elevations, however, the conditions in somewhat sheltered micro-environments are still severe and inhospitable for most plants.

A few of the plants discussed elsewhere in this book are occasionally found in sheltered areas above timberline, but they have been placed in other chapters because they usually grow well below timberline.

Above treeline, conditions Alpine
are cold wind and unfiltered sunshine.
To survive in the glare,
plants are covered with hair,
while down out of the wind they recline.

With its sprawling, ground-hugging, cushion-like form, Coville's phlox is typical of plants that grow on exposed, windswept ridges and flats above timberline. Its stems are **thick and woody**, but the **tiny, sticky-hairy, needle-like leaves** are clustered so tightly that the stems are rarely visible.

The 5-petaled, pinwheel-like flowers sit atop 1–3" stalks that project just above the cushion of leaves. The flowers are frequently so numerous and so densely packed that the leaves are completely covered. The resulting **low mound of solid white or pink or lavender blossoms** adds quite a spectacular touch of color to the often sparsely vegetated, rocky terrain. If you get close enough to this mound, you will notice a soft, delicious aroma.

Coville's phlox is given the scientific name *Phlox condensata*— a very appropriate species name indeed—in some books.

DRY FLATS ABOVE AND BELOW TIMBERLINE • WHITE, PINK, OR LAVENDER FLOWERS • 5 PETALS, UNITED IN A TUBE

ALPINE ADAPTATIONS: Dwarfed stature (1–3" tall); narrow leaves in a dense basal cushion; hairiness.
RANGE: Only in the mountains of California and Nevada.
TAHOE LOCATIONS: Common on dry, exposed ridges and slopes all the way from near lake level to 10,800'.

ALPINE CRYPTANTHA
Cryptantha humilis ∾ Borage Family

Like most members of the borage family, alpine cryptantha has five petals united into a tube that flares into a pinwheel and has a **raised ring around the throat** of the flower tube. Alpine cryptantha is unusual for a cryptantha, however, in that it has large flowers **and** a high-elevation habitat; of the many other Sierra Nevada cryptanthas, none shares both of these characteristics.

Alpine cryptantha's clusters of flowers rise on thick stems above soft, gray-green leaves. The large, bright, pure white flowers with yellow rings in their throats stand out in the austere, rocky environment above timberline—all the more for their relative rarity in Tahoe.

**ROCKY SLOPES ABOVE TIMBERLINE • WHITE FLOWERS
5 PETALS, UNITED IN A TUBE**

ALPINE ADAPTATIONS: Short stature (to 1' tall); hairiness.
RANGE: From the Sierra Nevada to Colorado in mid- to high elevations.
TAHOE LOCATIONS: Rare on rocky slopes above timberline.

CUT-LEAF DAISY
Erigeron compositus ∽ Sunflower Family

Cut-leaf daisy has the typical dwarfed form of an alpine plant, with a 2–3" stem, except that the flowerhead looks like it belongs on a 2–3' plant. The flowerhead is 1" or so across—nearly as large as the flower stem is tall. It consists of **20 to 50 white or pale purple ray flowers** (there is also a variety that has no rays) surrounding a **dense yellow 'button' of many disk flowers**. The small, lobed, mitten-like leaves form a dense mat that lies close to its rocky alpine 'soil.'

Cut-leaf daisy does grow below timberline, but it also reaches the summits of Tahoe's highest peaks.

Related plants: Another white daisy, but one of grassy meadows at lower elevations, is the much taller **Coulter's daisy** (*Erigeron coulteri*).

ROCKY ALPINE RIDGES • WHITE FLOWERHEADS
MANY RAY AND DISK FLOWERS

ALPINE ADAPTATIONS: Dwarfed stature (1–6" tall); narrow leaves; dense mat of basal leaves; hairiness.
RANGE: The Sierra Nevada to Alaska; east to the Rockies and Greenland.
TAHOE LOCATIONS: Occasional on rocky slopes and ridges from about 7500' to the summit of the highest Tahoe peak (Freel Peak) at 10,881'.

119

ALPINE GOLD, ALPINE HULSEA
Hulsea algida ∽ Sunflower Family

Alpine gold is one of the few Tahoe plants that occurs **only in the alpine environment above timberline** (though sometimes this is 'cold-induced' pseudo-alpine). Although it grows on wind-swept ridges and summits, it usually grows in relatively sheltered habitats behind rocks, and it is rather tall for an alpine plant, sometimes reaching over 1' high.

Alpine gold is a composite: each stem bears a **single, large (1–2" across), woolly flowerhead** that consists of **25 to 60 bright yellow ray flowers** surrounding a **yellow disk**. The narrow, toothed leaves are mostly basal, and they are covered with sticky, white hairs. The leaves have a strong, sweet aroma that you may not find altogether pleasant.

The genus *Hulsea* is named after G. W. Hulse, a 19th-century Army surgeon and botanist.

ROCKY RIDGES ABOVE TIMBERLINE
YELLOW FLOWERHEADS • MANY RAY AND DISK FLOWERS

ALPINE ADAPTATIONS: Short stature (4–15" tall); narrow, mostly basal leaves; dense hairiness.
RANGE: Among rocks on high, exposed ridges, from Mt. Whitney to Mt. Rose in the Sierra Nevada, and in the Rockies.
TAHOE LOCATIONS: Common at or near the summit of the highest peaks, from about 9500' to 10,881'.

With its low, matted form and finely hairy, tiny leaves, sulphur flower is ideally suited for the wind-swept ridges of the highest elevations above timberline. It is one of the more common of the alpine plants, but it is also frequently found all the way down to lake level (where it grows in a somewhat modified form—the flower stem is taller and the mat of leaves is much looser).

In the alpine version, **the large, spherical flowerhead of tiny, lemon-yellow flowers** rises only a few inches above the mat of spoon-shaped leaves. As with all buckwheats, the tiny flowers appear to have four or six papery petals, but if you look under these 'petals' you won't find any sepals—what appear to be petals are actually sepals (remember, the sepals are the outside layer in the bud, so all flowers have to have sepals). These showy flowers are often tinged with red, and they turn red or pink as they dry.

Related plants: Butterballs (*Eriogonum ovalifolium*) is another common buckwheat of alpine areas. It has balls of beige to pink flowers.

OPEN SLOPES ABOVE AND BELOW TIMBERLINE
YELLOW FLOWERS IN DENSE HEADS
4 OR 6 TINY 'PETALS' (ACTUALLY SEPALS)

ALPINE ADAPTATIONS: Dwarfed stature (4–6" tall); dense basal mat of small leaves; hairiness.
RANGE: Occurs from near sea level to 10,000' (a remarkable elevation range!) in California and Oregon and east to Colorado.
TAHOE LOCATIONS: Common on dry ridges from lake level to 10,000'.

ALPINE BUTTERCUP
Ranunculus eschscholtzii ∽ *Buttercup Family*

In the thin air and dry, rocky flats above timberline, the rocks are covered with rainbows of lichen—soft browns and greens, bright yellows and oranges, rich reds, and velvety blacks. Scattered among the rocks are occasional flowers snuggled close to the dry ground. The wind is whipping through you and howling in your frozen ears; you envy some of the flowers their sheltered niches. Then, like a cluster of golden suns come to warm you, the brilliant yellow blossoms of alpine buttercup peek out from their haven under a rock overhang.

As surprised as you may be to see buttercups up here, you will easily recognize them, for they have the typical **glossy yellow** buttercup flowers with **dense clusters of reproductive parts in their centers**. Unlike many buttercups, however, this alpine species has only five regular petals. The flowers rise 6" or so above 3-parted, shiny green leaves.

Though the genus name *Ranunculus* means 'little frog,' it probably doesn't refer to this particular species, which grows quite a distance from the nearest creek!

SHELTERED AREAS NEAR AND ABOVE TIMBERLINE
YELLOW FLOWERS • 5 (SOMETIMES MORE) SEPARATE PETALS

ALPINE ADAPTATIONS: Short stature (3–8" tall).
RANGE: At high elevations throughout the western mountains.
TAHOE LOCATIONS: Occasional on rocky flats near and above timberline, to about 10,600'.

LEMMON'S DRABA

Draba lemmonii ☞ *Mustard Family*

Lemmon's draba is easily identifiable as a mustard by its petal arrangement (**four in a cross**), its mustard-like taste, and its flattened seed pods. It is a small, hardy flower that grows to the summits of Tahoe's highest peaks. There are many alpine drabas, and they are difficult to distinguish from each other, but Lemmon's draba can be identified by its **twisted, hairy seed pods**. Its small flowers rise only 1–5" above the dense clusters of spoon-shaped, hairy basal leaves.

ROCKY RIDGES NEAR AND ABOVE TIMBERLINE
YELLOW FLOWERS • 4 SEPARATE PETALS

ALPINE ADAPTATIONS: Dwarfed stature (1–5" tall); dense mat of small basal leaves; hairiness.
RANGE: Endemic to the Sierra Nevada.
TAHOE LOCATIONS: Occasional in rock crevices and on open, rocky ridges near and above timberline (to the summit of the highest peak), from about 9000' to 10,881'.

SIBBALDIA
Sibbaldia procumbens ∞ *Rose Family*

Sibbaldia is an odd member of the 'quite normal' rose family (five uniform, regular petals), and it can **carpet large areas** (both above and below timberline) with its mats of **strawberry-like, wedge-shaped, 3-lobed leaves**. The five **narrow, yellow petals** are so **widely spaced** that the **larger green sepals** show through. It looks rather like the five tiny petals fell accidentally onto a green 'platform' (much as aspen leaves fall onto neighboring pines). The ground-hugging sibbaldia provides some fall color of its own, as its leaves turn copper red at the end of the blooming season.

Since it grows in areas of some moisture (usually areas covered by snow well into summer), sibbaldia is a reliable indicator of areas where snow lingers.

The genus *Sibbaldia* is named after R. Sibbald, a 17th-century Scottish naturalist and physician.

DAMPISH FLATS ABOVE AND BELOW TIMBERLINE
YELLOW FLOWERS • 5 SEPARATE PETALS

ALPINE ADAPTATIONS: Dwarfed stature (2–5" tall); carpet of basal leaves; hairiness.
RANGE: Circumboreal; in the western mountains from California to Alaska, across Canada to Greenland, and throughout northern Eurasia.
TAHOE LOCATIONS: Uncommon on damp ridges and meadows of late-lying snow from about 7500' to 10,000'.

DUSTY MAIDEN
DOUGLAS PINCUSHION, CHAENACTIS
Chaenactis douglasii var. *rubricaulis*
Sunflower Family

Like thistles (p. 87), dusty maiden is a dry-environment composite that has **only disk flowers**. Dusty maiden, however, is a much smaller and softer-looking plant than a thistle: the small flowerheads have many tiny, non-spiny tubular flowers; the leaves (mostly basal) are white-woolly and finely divided like lace. Close inspection of one of the **rose-tinted, greenish-yellow disk flowers** will show a tiny, 5-petaled star at the end of a narrow tube, from which protrudes a needle-like stigma that is split into two gracefully arching segments. The overall effect is somewhat reminiscent of a pin-cushion.

Dusty maiden is unusual in that it grows all the way from foothill elevations to above timberline. As you would expect, its gets smaller and more compact as it goes higher.

DRY FLATS ABOVE AND BELOW TIMBERLINE
PINK FLOWERHEADS • MANY DISK FLOWERS

ALPINE ADAPTATIONS: Short stature (4–12" tall), narrowly lobed, mostly basal leaves; gray-green 'felt' covering leaves.
RANGE: The Sierra Nevada (mostly the eastern slopes) to Oregon; east to Colorado.
TAHOE LOCATIONS: Common on dry flats from lake level to about 10,000'.

WHITNEY'S LOCOWEED
Astragalus whitneyi ∞ *Pea Family*

The pale pink or purple (sometimes white) flowers of this alpine plant are easily identifiable as pea flowers by their 'banner and keel' form (see glossary). The small flowers grow in clusters along a short, decumbent stem, while the equally small, finely divided leaflets grow in several opposite pairs along their own stem. The flowers, though delicately beautiful, 'pale' in comparison to the **dramatic and bizarre seedpods, which are swollen, golden, red-mottled, 1–2" long 'sausages.'** Late in the fall, when the seeds and the pods have dried, you can make an eerie 'death-rattle' by giving the pod a slight shake.

The common name 'locoweed' refers to the effect this plant has on many species of animals—the optic nerve is 'poisoned,' causing objects to appear distorted and enlarged. The spooked animal soon goes 'loco'!

ROCKY FLATS AT AND BELOW TIMBERLINE
PINK, PURPLE, OR WHITE FLOWERS
5 SEPARATE PETALS, IN AN IRREGULAR PEA FLOWER

ALPINE ADAPTATIONS: Dwarfed stature (3–6" tall); loose mat of narrow basal leaves; hairiness.
RANGE: Only in the Sierra Nevada and the high deserts of the Great Basin to the east.
TAHOE LOCATIONS: Fairly common on dry, gravelly ridges and flats from about 8000' to 10,500'.

Dwarf alpine daisy is another of the few Tahoe plants that **occur only in alpine environments**. It grows in the protection of rock crevices or among rocks on open, windswept ridges to the summits of Tahoe's highest peaks. The narrow basal leaves of dwarf alpine daisy hug the ground in a dense mat, from which rise the tiny, 1–3" stems. The stem and leaves are covered with fine, white hairs. Each stem bears a solitary **composite** flowerhead with 15 to 35 narrow **lavender-purple ray flowers** surrounding a loose, **yellow disk**.

**ROCKY RIDGES AND SUMMITS OF HIGH ALPINE
PURPLE-LAVENDER FLOWERHEADS
MANY RAY AND DISK FLOWERS**

ALPINE ADAPTATIONS: Dwarfed stature (1–3" tall); mat of narrow basal leaves; hairiness.
RANGE: Only on high peaks in the Sierra Nevada, from Mt. Whitney to Mt. Rose.
TAHOE LOCATIONS: Occasional on and near the summit of only two peaks (Freel Peak and Mt. Rose), from about 10,000' to 10,881'.

LYALL'S LUPINE
Lupinus lyallii ❦ *Pea Family*

 With its distinctive 'banner and keel' flowers, pea-like pods, and palmately compound leaves, Lyall's lupine is clearly in the pea family and clearly a lupine. Like most lupines, **its flowers are predominantly blue with white markings**. Unlike its lower-elevation relatives, however, Lyall's lupine is a dwarfed, ground-hugging plant. Its whorls of leaflets, which are densely covered with silky, white hairs, form small 5- or 6-fingered hands.

 Lyall's lupine is given the scientific name *Lupinus lepidus* var. *lobbii* in some books.

 Related plants: Of the many Tahoe lupines of lower elevations, the tall, blue-flowered **broad-leaf lupine** (*L. polyphyllus*) of wet areas is probably the most conspicuous.

DRY RIDGES ABOVE AND BELOW TIMBERLINE • BLUE FLOWERS
5 SEPARATE PETALS, IN AN IRREGULAR PEA FLOWER

ALPINE ADAPTATIONS: Dwarfed stature (2–5" tall); narrow basal leaves; hairiness.
RANGE: At high elevations from the Sierra Nevada to Washington.
TAHOE LOCATIONS: Common on dry ridges from about 7500' to 10,500'.

DAVIDSON'S PENSTEMON, ALPINE PENSTEMON
Penstemon davidsonii ∾ Snapdragon Family

This marvelous penstemon is one of the most striking of Tahoe's alpine wildflowers, both for its **rich purple color** and for the almost incongruously **large size of its blossoms**. Its typical, tubular, penstemon flowers (1–2" long) look immense on their dwarfed, 4–6" stems, especially in contrast to the ground-hugging mat of tiny, oval, evergreen leaves. The three petals of the lower lip, the anthers, and the antherless staminode all are white-woolly.

Davidson's penstemon sometimes hybridizes with one of its lower-elevation relatives (mountain pride, p. 38) in the small elevational range where both species occur.

ROCKY RIDGES NEAR AND ABOVE TIMBERLINE
PURPLE FLOWERS • 5 PETALS, UNITED IN A 2-LIPPED TUBE

ALPINE ADAPTATIONS: Dwarfed stature (4–6" tall); basal mat of small, fleshy leaves; hairiness.
RANGE: At high elevations from the Sierra Nevada to Washington.
TAHOE LOCATIONS: Occasional among rocks near and above timberline, to the summit of Tahoe's highest peaks, from about 9500' to 10,881'.

QUICK IDENTIFICATION TABLE

COLOR	APPARENT NUMBER AND FORM OF PETALS	
	5 SEPARATE	**5 UNITED IN BOWL, URN, TRUMPET, CROWN**
WHITE	Wintergreen, 15	Pinedrops, 14
	Pipsissewa, 16	Buckbean, 43
	Miner's lettuce, 29	Ballhead gilia, 88
	Alum-root, 30	Manzanita, 94
	Cinquefoil, 32	Alpine gentian, 99
	Aquatic buttercup, 42	Hesperochiron, 101
	Sundew, 43	Nemophila, 101
	Macloskey's violet, 49	Alpine heather, 108
	Grass-of-Parnassus, 51	Huckleberry, 108
	Mitrewort, 52	Phlox, 117
	Saxifrage, 52	Cryptantha, 118
	Chickweed, 56	
	Toad lily, 57	
	Spring beauty, 57	
	Whitethorn, 94	
	Tobacco brush, 94	
	Woodland star, 98	
	Thimbleberry, 109	
YELLOW/ ORANGE	Cinquefoil, 32	Stonecrop, 33
	Mountain violet, 93	Collomia, 80
	St. John's wort, 103	
	Tinker's penny, 103	
	Alpine buttercup, 122	
	Sibbaldia, 124	
RED/PINK/ RED-PURPLE	Columbine, 21	Wintergreen, 15
	Alum-root, 30	Snowplant, 22
	Primrose, 37	Whisker brush, 80
	Purple cinquefoil, 45	Bridge's gilia, 81
	Spring beauty, 57	Scarlet gilia, 88
	Checkermallow, 86	Snowberry, 102
	Beckwith violet, 93	Red heather, 108
	Rose, 109	Bog laurel, 108
	Spiraea, 109	Phlox, 117
	Strawberry, 109	
	Avens, 110	
MAROON/ BROWN	Beckwith violet, 93	Twinberry, 102
BLUE/BLUE- PURPLE	Monkshood, 70	Gentian, 68
	Larkspur, 70	Polemonium, 69
	Blue flax, 91	Waterleaf, 89
	Violet, 93	Phacelia, 90
	Squaw carpet, 94	Stickseed, 92
		Nightshade, 95

APPARENT NUMBER AND FORM OF PETALS

5 UNITED IN 2-LIPPED TUBE	4	VARIABLE NUMBER (5–20)
Pennyroyal, 79	Shieldleaf, 29 Steershead, 31 Corydalis, 58 Watercress, 78 Deer's tongue, 99	Anemone, 26 Marsh marigold, 55 Lewisia, 57 Hesperochiron, 101
Lousewort, 20 Monkeyflower, 62 Broomrape, 64 Owlsclover, 82 Paintbrush, 107	Suncup, 35 Evening-primrose, 76 Wallflower, 78 Draba, 123	Pond-lily, 44 Buttercup, 55
Mountain pride, 38 Elephantheads, 61 Horse-mint, 79 Pennyroyal, 79 Owlsclover, 82 Monkeyflower, 83 Paintbrush, 106–7	Shieldleaf, 29 Steershead, 31 Rosy sedum, 34 Fuchsia, 35 Rock fringe, 36 Fireweed, 36 Corydalis, 58 Shooting star, 63 Dagger pod, 78	
		Peony, 112
Penstemon, 38, 129 Broomrape, 64 Veronica, 67 Porterella, 71 Downingia, 71 Self-heal, 113	Veronica, 67 Gentian, 68	

QUICK IDENTIFICATION TABLE

COLOR	APPARENT NUMBER AND FORM OF PETALS	
	SUNFLOWER: RAYS AND DISK OR RAYS ONLY	SUNFLOWER: DISK ONLY
WHITE	Cut-leaf daisy, 119 Coulter's daisy, 119	Thistle, 87
YELLOW/ ORANGE	Mule ears, 77 Balsamroot, 77 Mountain dandelion, 85 Arnica, 104 Alpine gold, 120	
RED/PINK/ RED-PURPLE	Stephanomeria, 85	Eupatorium, 39 Thistle, 87 Dusty maiden, 125
MAROON/ BROWN		
BLUE/BLUE-PURPLE	Alpine daisy, 127	

APPARENT NUMBER AND FORM OF PETALS

3 OR 6	TINY PETALS: FLOWERS IN CLUSTERS OR HEADS	PEA LIKE: BANNER, WINGS AND KEEL
Coralroot, 17	Buckwheat 27	
Twayblade, 17	Dirty socks, 27	
Star tulip, 18	Mountain sorrel, 28	
Duck potato, 42	Cow parsnip, 50	
Rein orchid, 53	Ranger's buttons, 50	
Bog orchid, 53	Angelica, 50	
Corn lily, 54	Lovage, 50	
Death camas, 65	Elderberry, 102	
Mariposa lily, 74	Butterballs, 121	
Hyacinth brodiaea, 75		
Sierra red onion, 84		
Washington lily, 100		
Tiger lily, 60	Sulphur flower, 121	
Pretty face, 75		
Fritillary, 105		
Sierra onion, 84	Butterballs, 121	Locoweed, 126
Fritillary, 111		
Fritillary, 105		
Camas lily, 65		Locoweed, 126
Blue-eyed grass, 66		Lupine, 128
Onion, 84		

GLOSSARY

I have taken care to limit the use of botanical terms to a minimum, using non-technical alternatives when possible. The following terms probably need to be defined, although most of them are defined as they are used in the text.

anther: the pollen-producing tip of the male part of a flower.

annual: living only one year, having to start over each year from seed.

axil: where the leaf stalk joins the plant stem.

banner: the upper petal of a pea flower.

basal leaves: leaves located at the base of the stem.

bracts: leaf-like structures performing different functions than leaves, e.g., the upper 'leaves' in a paintbrush, which have adapted to look like petals.

calyx: collective term for the sepals.

chaparral: evergreen shrubs adapted to dry environments and fire.

circumboreal: occurring around the globe in high latitudes.

composite flower: consisting of many separate flowers in a tight head, usually appearing to be one many-petaled flower, such as a daisy.

corolla: collective term for the petals.

cushion plant: a plant of the alpine zone with densely packed, ground-hugging leaves.

disk flower: in the sunflower (composite) family, the small, tubular flowers comprising the 'button' in the center of the flowerhead; some composites only have disk flowers.

endemic: confined to a certain region, e.g., a Sierra endemic is found only in the Sierra Nevada.

filament: the stalk of the male part of a flower, which bears the anther at its tip.

glaucous: covered with a fine, whitish powder.

inferior ovary: an ovary situated below the petals.

keel: the lower two petals cradling the reproductive parts in pea flowers, somewhat resembling the keel of a boat.

leaflet: one of the segments of a compound leaf.

life zone: one of the divisions of a zonation system based on temperature used to describe and explain the occurrence of different kinds of plants in different latitudes or at different elevations within the same latitude.

mat plant: a plant with loosely packed, ground-hugging leaves, not as dense as a cushion plant.

micro-environment: the environment in the immediate vicinity of a plant (e.g., wet, dry, rocky, shady).

monocotyledon: a plant with only one embryonic leaf, easily identified in the mature plant by its three or six petals and its grass-like leaves.

mycotrophic: obtaining nutrients from fungi attached to a plant's roots.

nitrogen-fixing: the ability to convert nitrogen in the air to usable soil nitrogen (such as in peas).

opposite leaves: leaf arrangement in which two leaves branch off a stem from opposite sides of the same point.

palmately compound: having leaflets all arising from the same point (like the fingers of the hand).

parasite: obtaining food and nutrients from living organisms.

pedicel: a flower stalk.

perennial: living for more than one year; usually the rootstalk remains when the above-ground part of the plant dies back in the winter.

petaloid: resembling a petal, usually referring to a sepal that is colorful like a petal (such as in most flowers of the lily family).

petiole: a leaf stalk.

phyllary: one of the narrow, green bracts forming the cup of the flowerhead in a member of the sunflower family.

pistil: the female part, including the ovary, style, and stigma.

ray flowers: the wide-flaring flowers (rays) of members of the sunflower family; what you may think are the petals in a daisy.

rosette: a crowded whorl of basal leaves.

saprophyte: obtaining food and nutrients from dead and decaying organic matter.

scree: a slope or field of small rocks.

sepal: the usually green part of the flower beneath the petals, forming the outer protective layer in the bud.

stamen: the male structure, including the anther and the filament.

staminode: a sterile stamen (such as in penstemons).

stigma: the tip of the female part that is receptive to pollen.

style: the thin stalk connecting the ovary and the stigma of the female structure.

succulent: fleshy, thick, and juicy; usually referring to leaves that hold water.

superior ovary: an ovary that is situated above the petals.

talus: a slope or field of large rocks.

timberline: the highest elevation at which trees can still grow.

umbel: a flower arrangement in which the flower stems all radiate out from the same point, like the spokes of an umbrella.

wings: the two lateral petals in flowers of the pea family, usually cradling the keel.

SELECT REFERENCES

Armstrong, W. 1979. Seldom-seen parasitic flowers. *Pacific Discovery* 32(6):10–17.

Bailey, L. 1963. *How Plants Get Their Names.* Dover Press, New York.

Barbour, M., and J. Major, eds. 1977. *Terrestrial Vegetation of California.* Wiley and Sons, New York.

Carville, J. 1989. *Lingering in Tahoe's Wildflower Gardens.* Mountain Gypsy Press, Chicago Park, California.

Crittenson, M., and D. Telfer. 1975. *Wildflowers of the West.* Celestial Arts, Millbrae, California.

Grant, V. 1952. Isolation and hybridization between *Aquilegia formosa* and *A. pubescens. El Aliso* 2(4).

Hickman, J., ed. 1993. *The Jepson Manual of Higher Plants of California.* University of California Press, Berkeley.

Hood, M., and B. Hood. 1969. *Yosemite Wildflowers.* Flying Spur Press, Yosemite, California.

Horn, E. 1976. *Wildflowers 3: The Sierra Nevada.* Touchstone Press, Beaverton, Oregon.

Macior, L. 1977. The pollination ecology of *Pedicularis* in the Sierra Nevada. *Bulletin of the Torrey Botanical Club* 104(2).

Manning, H. 1979. *Mountain Flowers of the Cascades and Olympics.* The Mountaineers, Seattle.

Munz, P. 1963. *California Mountain Wildflowers.* University of California Press, Berkeley.

Munz, P. 1968. *A California Flora.* University of California Press, Berkeley.

Niehaus, T., and C. Ripper. 1976. *A Field Guide to Pacific States Wildflowers.* Houghton Mifflin, Boston.

Parsons, D. 1976. Chaparral. *Pacific Discovery* 29(2):21–27.

Proctor, M., and P. Yeo. 1972. *The Pollination of Flowers.* Taplinger Publishing Co., New York.

Smiley, F. 1915. The alpine and subalpine vegetation of the Lake Tahoe region. *Botanical Gazette* 59(4):265–86.

Smith, G. 1973. A flora of the Tahoe Basin and neighboring areas. *The Wasmann Journal of Biology* 31(1):1–231.

Spellenberg, R. 1979. *The Audubon Society Field Guide to North American Wildflowers.* Alfred A. Knopf, New York.

Storer, T., and R. Usinger. 1963. *Sierra Nevada Natural History.* University of California Press, Berkeley.

Weeden, N. 1981. *Sierra Nevada Flora.* Wilderness Press, Berkeley.

Whitney, S. 1979. *A Sierra Club Naturalist's Guide to the Sierra Nevada.* Sierra Club Books, San Francisco.

Zwinger, A., and B. Willard. 1972. *Land Above the Trees.* Harper and Row, New York.

INDEXES

PLANT FAMILIES

COMMON NAMES

Names in **boldface** type refer to species given primary treatments.

SCIENTIFIC NAMES

Names in **boldface** type refer to species given primary treatments.

ABOUT THE AUTHOR

Laird R. Blackwell, who received his Ph.D. from Stanford University, has lived and studied in the Sierra Nevada for over 20 years. His passion for the high mountains and their wildflowers has taken him hiking, backpacking, photographing, and botanizing in the mountains of the American West, Alaska, Hawaii, Switzerland, Scotland, New Zealand, and Guatemala.

Laird lives at Lake Tahoe, where he is professor and Chairman of Humanities at Sierra Nevada College. He teaches courses in Ecology, Psychology, Literature, and Mythology. To him, wildflowers are nature's poetry, and they offer us a path into the deeper layers of our psyches.

Laird and his wife Melinda, who is a high-school English teacher, lead ecology and wildflower field trips in Tahoe, Mt. Rainier, Yosemite and other mountain areas in the West.